D0049205

DEAD
RECKONING

DEAD RECKONING

Navigating a Life on the Last Frontier, Courting Tragedy on Its High Seas

DAVE ATCHESON

Skyhorse Publishing

Skyhorse Publishing books may be purchased in bulk at special discounts for sales promotion, corporate gifts, fund-raising, or educational purposes. Special editions can also be created to specifications. For details, contact the Special Sales Department, Skyhorse Publishing, 307 West 36th Street, 11th Floor, New York, NY 10018 or info@skyhorsepublishing.com.

Skyhorse® and Skyhorse Publishing® are registered trademarks of Skyhorse Publishing, Inc.®, a Delaware corporation.

www.skyhorsepublishing.com

10 9 8 7 6 5 4 3 2 1

Library of Congress Cataloging-in-Publication Data is available on file.

ISBN: 978-1-62873-681-6
Ebook ISBN: 978-1-62914-024-7

Printed in the United States of America

This book is dedicated to all the men and women who seek a different path in life and those who choose to make their living on the sea. It is also dedicated to my family, my sister Leanne and her son Jack; my brother Gordon and his family; Marylou, and my dad, George Atcheson, who has always been there for me and encouraged me to seek out the path less traveled; and for Cindy Detrow, for being there and encouraging me now, with all my love.

CONTENTS

INTRODUCTION

As a herring fisherman in the early 1990s, I didn't know I was participating in one of the deadliest fisheries in Alaska, second only to crabbing. But most of us who fish for a living are either not aware of these figures or don't dwell on them, otherwise we might be less inclined to choose it as a vocation. Most of us started out young, longing for adventure and feeling infallible, often falling into a routine, trading long stretches of incredibly hard work for the luxury of month upon month off in a row.

Like most fishermen, my life intersected with those who had known or had been involved in tragedy. While working for a sea-food company, buying herring, I found myself aboard a boat that had lost a crewman during the recent crab season. A solemn pall had been cast over the entire vessel; it was conspicuously quiet both at mealtimes and in the cabin I shared with the deckhand who had lost his grip on his crewmate as a wave washed over the boat. This deckhand kept his nose constantly in the Bible as he went somberly about his duties while the rest of the crew tried, without hope, to ignore the loss and get on with their season and their lives.

There was also the *St. George*, on which I'd caught a brief ride to the herring grounds. The following winter they would vanish on the Bering Sea, the only trace of their existence being a small life raft found floundering empty in the open sea. Initially, those familiar with the well-kept boat and experienced crew assured family and friends they'd be found. But as hours churned slowly into days, and days into weeks, it became painfully obvious that the raft would remain the only remnant of the 94-foot vessel and its six-man crew.

It's something you don't think could happen to you—at least, not at first. Still, for every sinking, every catastrophe, every reported mishap, an untold number of near-misses speak to the contrary— brief moments of terror that could easily turn out to be links in hor- rific chain-reactions that never materialize. They are what my fellow deckhand, Karl, would refer to as "Oh Shit Moments," after which there's usually a pause to ever so briefly consider your fate before going back about the work of hauling gear or securing a catch. Once in a while, however, they do turn into lengthy ordeals that extend well beyond the Oh Shit Moment into hours of terror. This is the story of those perils that go unreported, of those moments and the many in between—often filled with camaraderie and good fortune—that make up an adventure at sea and, over time, fashion who each of us becomes on a much larger scale.

It's also the story of a young kid from a sleepy Northeastern col- lege town, where nothing ever seemed to happen, who ventured into the always unpredictable torrent of life on "The Last Frontier." It is a world away even from the confines of Anchorage, the state's urban center and a bustling modern metropolis. It's the old Alaska, peppered with the new, and in truth as bizarre, as beautiful, and as extreme as that painted by any work of fiction. It thrives on the docks and waterfronts, beyond the tourist traps and cruise ships moored in our smallest fishing towns, a realm often peopled by those who are searching for something, as well as those who shun, or at least tend to question society. It's a place where college stu- dents and "fish hippies" work in canneries alongside survivalists, rednecks, and religious freaks. Where deckhands who suffer from "Seasonal Work Syndrome" slave all summer long in order to have the entire winter to relax if they so choose, or to feed their insa- tiable appetites for adventure—skiing glaciers, climbing mountains, or traveling to some far-off, exotic, and cheap land. This is a story, and a place, in which many of today's deeply ingrained ideas of success and status constantly come into question. Where, for me, the resulting conflict would finally resolve itself in the least likely of places: on the Bering Sea, aboard a boat in peril, during a night of terror that would reshape the lives of everyone involved—for some of us drastically and incontrovertibly altering the very way we view the world and acknowledge our places in it.

PREFACE

SERENDIPITY

SOLDOTNA, MAY 1997

It was as if I were walking through a lingering internal mist, a quiet euphoria I imagine is felt by soldiers returning from battle. Completely in the here and now, safe for the time being and untouchable. As if nothing could disturb me.

This sustained feeling of resignation and well-being had been with me since stepping ashore a few days before, and now it followed as I went about my business. We'd left for the fishing grounds still in the throes of winter, and returned to a changed world—spring suddenly in full bloom and with it people possessed by the season, refreshed and invigorated. But I felt as if I moved just a few steps shy of everyone else—more deliberately, as if both with them and outside of them at the same time.

It was strange entering the service station. Someone at the counter was talking with an older man, the attendant or owner, about fishing. The older guy interrupted their chat just long enough to tell me to have a seat, that they were running behind. "You know how it is," he said, "everyone's in a hurry this time of year."

Not me.

Someone could have spit in my face and I would probably have just wiped it off and sat down. I could have waited forever, content to just sit there in the waiting area for my snow tires to come off, burying my gaze in an old magazine, picking up stray bits and pieces of conversation cast over the din of the shop. They were trading stories, new and old. The owner was complaining about fish prices. "They're not what they used to be," he said. "It's hardly worth going through all that crap, especially when I hear what happened to you."

I strained to listen but could pick up very little until the owner said something about Togiak, which sits on the shores of Bristol Bay, and I gathered that the customer and I had just returned from the same place. Falling in and then back out of their conversation, I caught a word here and there, diverting my attention from magazine shots of sports cars and souped-up trucks.

The owner said something about knowing where to set your gear. The customer argued and refuted the point, saying it was calm and that they thought they had lots of time. "We didn't think we'd get in trouble," he said.

"You never do," countered the owner.

The customer said something else, about having a hell of a trip, a nightmare he called it.

He wasn't the only one. I wondered what had happened to this guy. What reaction had he encountered upon returning home?

It was weird how people who had just heard about *our* ordeal had been coming up and hugging me. The woman I worked with occasionally at the local coffee shop, who fished commercially and had told me about the job in Bristol Bay—she had almost taken it herself—had thrown her arms around me and told me she didn't know what she would have done if I hadn't come back. But I was a couple of weeks removed from the incident and could hardly comprehend these reactions, especially now, back in Soldotna and in this odd void in which I found myself floating.

My glance fell back to the magazine and slid over the glossy ice cubes anchoring a glass of whiskey or down the lean, silky leg of a supermodel. But just as quickly, something pulled me back into the conversation.

The shop had gone quiet and the customer had become animated, the lines on his face—only slightly older than mine—flexing, an immediacy in his voice suddenly coming to bear. "The problem was," he said, his tone fervent and rising, "there was only one tender and we couldn't unload all our fish. So we sat there for hours with them in the net waiting for another boat. Then it got dark and there was a tide change, and that's when things got bad."

Then he mentioned something else, something strange. Did I even hear him right? Was he even talking about this season, or something in the distant past? Could he have said Cape Pierce? Either way, by this point it was impossible to hold out any longer.

"Where were you fishing?"

"Togiak," the customer said as I approached.

"Just got back from there myself," I said, trying to sound amiable. "I had a pretty bad time of it. Sounds like you did too."

"You could say that," he replied, almost as a challenge or maybe he was just skeptical, as if nothing could possibly match his story— what he'd been through.

"Did you lose a big set or something?" asked the owner, trying to be polite.

"We did," I said. "We almost lost everything, and had a couple unbelievable days afterward, and one hell of a long boat trip home."

The customer's eyes suddenly narrowed, almost examining me, looking deep to see if I was for real.

"We made a set way out too," I continued, "probably where we shouldn't have, and couldn't unload our catch. Sounds kinda like what happened to you."

"Sounds *exactly* like what happened us."

"Where were you?" I asked.

"Off of Cape Pierce."

So, I had heard correctly, but was momentarily dumbfounded, just trying to piece it all together.

"What boat?" I finally asked.

"The *Sea Mist*."

"What?"

"The *Sea Mist*," he repeated. "You know it?"

For a few long seconds all I could manage was stunned silence.

"I was on the *Iliamna Bay*," I whispered.

Suddenly the same long look of disbelief, of complete disassociation, fell over his entire body, shoulders and features sagging as he was thrown into the same stupor I'd just momentarily emerged from. That's when I first took notice of his lanky frame and clean-shaven face, and was instantly thrown back in time, returning for a moment to the cold chill and precarious pitch and heave of the deck that night, trying amidst the chaos and the shadow of halogen lights to decipher which one of those dark figures he was, hooded and wide-eyed and cast in the pall of eerie disaster.

Members of both the *Rafferty* and *Sea Mist* crews were there. They were the boats we co-oped with, working together during the openings, sharing our catch and profits in an effort to take a little bit of the gamble out of the game. We'd even tied up together a few nights. But crews kind of stick together, and guys look different out there, dirty and draped in raingear, seawater dripping from scruffy beards.

Then a smile slowly washed over his face as he began to fully comprehend the odd little turn our lives had just taken.

"That's right," I said, "we were on deck together."

"Holy shit, I really can't believe it. Greg," he said, holding out his hand. "I was first over from the *Sea Mist*."

"I think I remember now, you were there pretty much the whole time," I said. "I'm glad to see you," I stammered. "Glad we all made it home."

"Any one of us might not have. One of your guys, though, the one that got yanked, he almost didn't."

Slowly raising my thumb, I pointed like a hitchhiker at myself.

"That was me," I said.

"Oh my God," he muttered, reaching out all at once and taking my hand, shaking it for a long while as his other hand clasped my shoulder. I grabbed his arm in what was close to an embrace and felt something significant pass between us. Though we barely knew one another, we shared what no one else had: a bond that we barely understood and that certainly no else could—unless, of course, they'd been there with us on the Bering Sea that night. Even if we never crossed paths again it was something we would always share.

When I left I thought to myself again how much I liked this feeling, this steady, impenetrable sense of complacency, and hoped it would stay. Nothing could possibly bother me. It sounded somehow like invincibility, but that was hardly it—for I knew, now more than ever, that I could be taken down in an instant. But for the time being that hardly mattered. That was just the point—nothing mattered, not as much as being here now, in the moment and only in the moment.

TIME TO FLEE (INTO BATTLE)

SOLDOTNA, MARCH 1997

I'D BEEN IN town far too long. Six months of slinging mochas to high schools girls and lattes to local business people was getting old. I'd tried to stay put before—at one point even made it to assistant manager, learned everything there was to know about roasting, brewing, and serving coffee. The job was a good fit, at least in the winter, because I like coffee—love it, as a matter of fact. Yet when the weather would start to turn and I'd hear the fishing was good, or later on when someone would call and tell me how much money they were bringing in, it was inevitable: I'd have to catch the next boat out and reap the rewards of the end of the season. Living by the tides, picking fish, not returning to my recurring role at the coffee shop until the fishing was long over and my earnings nearly spent.

One of my colleagues at the coffee shop told me about the job on the *Iliamna Bay*. In the summer, Marion fished a setnet site with her partner, but like me, she pumped shots of espresso to make it through the winter. She had intended to take the job herself but at the last minute decided not to. She referred me to Karl, who, like a lot of off-duty and out-of-work fishermen, hung out at the joint for hours on end. He was familiar to me—a family man in his early thirties with dusty hair. He owned a local setnet operation and made money in the interim deckhanding for halibut boats. Apparently, for the last several years, he worked as the skiff man—kind of an upper-tier position running a small boat that attaches to one end of the net when a seiner (in this case the *Iliamna Bay*) encircles a school of fish.

Like most jobs as deckhands, one often hears of them through the grapevine, and Karl was my contact. Karl talked to the captain, and afterward almost assured me I'd have the last spot on the boat. Of course, there was still the process of the introduction: the ceremonial meeting of the skipper. This process is much less formal than a regular job interview; questions and answers are usually traded over a cup of coffee or a drink, and the decision to hire based entirely upon the captain's gut. While today many herring fisheries are co-opted among all the participating boats, herring fishing in the late nineties was one of the last free-for-alls, and although I'd previously worked aboard tenders, which mainly entailed sitting around waiting before pumping fish aboard to be hauled, this time I was looking forward to being in the thick of it. Seining was the real battle for big money. To the uninitiated, it might resemble naval combat directly out of a World War II movie—a contest in which boats vie for position, usually in a small bay, while nearly as many spotter planes (one- or two-passenger aircraft circling clockwise), relay information such as where the schools of fish are and precisely where nets should be set. Meanwhile, tenders—the large collection vessels that transport fish back to the canneries—loom in the distance. Giant and lumbering, they wait for their assigned fishing boat to finish making a set; when this happens, the tenders carefully motor in, negotiating a web of outstretched nets, and sometimes a maze of rocks, in order to pump aboard—if the fishing is good—hundreds of tons of herring. Mass quantities of this small fish are then shipped to shore- and ocean-based processing facilities throughout the state of Alaska, and later on to Japan, where a premium is paid for the herring's golden caviar.

What made the process all the more exciting was the anticipation. It might take almost a week to reach the fishing grounds, and then days or even weeks while the Department of Fish and Game took samples to see if the roe was "ripe." The Department walked a tightrope, trying to determine the exact time the fish were ready to spawn and the eggs would be the tastiest. That's when they would call for an opening and the insanity would begin. A countdown and the jockeying for position, and then just twenty minutes of fishing!—enough time for fishermen to make just one set with their 600-foot seines. With the possibility of the herring quota being filled after only a couple of openings, it was one of the biggest gambles in fishing. Once a certain number of herring were caught you were done, your boat's chances for the year used up, along with all its supplies and thousands upon thousands of gallons of fuel, not to mention the crew's incredible outlay of time and effort.

2

THE USUAL NERVES

HOMER, APRIL 1997

IT WAS A two-hour drive south through a string of villages. Some had names that derived from ancient native dialects—Kasilof and Ninilchik. Others, like Anchor Point, were named by early explorers, in its case by Captain Cook, who happened to lose an anchor there. None were completely free from the grip of winter. Patches of dirty snow clung to the ground amidst the standing water and mud of "break-up"—the drab half-frozen period, and Alaska's fifth season that lingers long after winter and precedes spring.

Although it was initially liberating to leave the ties of my regular, albeit intermittent job, slowly a tightness began to settle deep in the pit of my stomach. The feeling of unease reached its pinnacle as I rounded the ridge above the town of Homer—the surrounding mountains and incredible stretch of open ocean suddenly presenting itself in its untamed vastness. There was nothing sinister or foreboding about this tense feeling. In fact, it was nothing out of the ordinary—just the same unrest that always presented itself as a prelude to any long voyage. And in no way did it resemble fear. After all, I'd worked on many boats and had my share of "Oh Shit Moments," and although I was well aware of what could happen out there, I hadn't quite reached the point where I really thought it could happen to me.

What was happening now was something less dramatic and more immediate: a little touch of apprehension based on what I knew was coming. The complete loss of freedom, the tight quarters, the stink of dirty socks, and the unknown—specifically, the personalities I'd have to deal with. When aboard a boat, crammed into a 300-square-foot cabin with three other people, a deckhand must be hyperaware of his crewmates and their quirks and must be that much more considerate, or living together—or more importantly, working together—just won't work. Most good skippers must have a bit of the armchair psychologist in them. While finding someone hardy enough to handle the physical labor required is critically important, they also look for deckhands of even temperament—at least while they are at sea. It doesn't matter how much work a deckhand does; a bad attitude can quickly infect an entire crew, causing everything to unravel and work to become even more arduous, sometimes even to the point of grinding to a near standstill. But maintaining an even temperament at sea is part of the reason why fishermen have the reputation for such explosive behavior once on shore. Even the most mellow, well-adjusted deckhand must have a release.

Rounding the top of that hill, all I could do was try to swallow my tension and hope for the best. After all, I hardly knew Karl and hadn't even met Brad, the other deckhand. And I'd only been introduced to our skipper, Tim, once, and it was difficult to gauge just where he stood on the dictatorial scale. Every skipper is different, every boat a world unto itself. A boat is a small self-contained empire run by an exalted ruler—some benevolent and others not.

No, this usual flurry of nerves welled-up every time, fueled by past experience, dating back to my first boat, the *Lancer*, after which it was a wonder I ever went back aboard another boat and out to sea again.

3

WELCOME ABOARD

ILIAMNA BAY, APRIL 1997

IT HAD BEEN nearly thirteen years since I'd gone out on my first trip, and walking down the dock in Homer toward Tim's boat I was still wondering—did I want to be a fisherman? For lack of anything else I was, and despite the knot of nerves in my stomach, at least this time I wasn't entering a completely alien world. After all these years I even looked the part, wearing broken-in Xtra-tuf boots, Grundens slung over my shoulder. More than that, I knew what I was getting into and that I could do the job. I also knew many of the other fishermen. It was very early in the season and there were only locals on the docks. Most were family men or second- or third-generation fishermen, some who skippered the boats their fathers had owned. Most were professionals and could not afford to live—or had lived through and recovered from—the reckless, easy-come-easy-go life that had been the downfall of many first time fishermen.

I made my way to the *Iliamna Bay,* where it was lined up with other seiners. At forty-two feet, it was definitely not the largest of the bunch. It would indeed be a tight journey, first to an opening in Cook Inlet before a five day haul out west, through the Aleutian Islands and on to the Bering Sea, all on our way to Bristol Bay. The *Iliamna Bay* was an older vessel, but in tip-top shape. I would later find out that the skipper, Tim, was an inveterate tinkerer and one-time mechanic, who took great pride in the condition of his boat.

I first saw Karl stacking some line on deck, and then Tim—
no doubt fresh from checking the engine. With barely time for a
greeting, I joined the flow of work, helping Karl tote gear from
Tim's truck onto the boat and finishing up various duties on deck.
We stopped briefly when Brad arrived with another truckload of
various tools and dry goods from last season that Tim had stored in
his shop over the winter.

Brad was a bit younger than the rest of us, probably in his late
twenties, with shoulder length hair and a freshly shaven face. He
had worked on Tim's boat for most of last year's salmon season.
Fairly new to Alaska and to fishing, he hadn't experienced anything
like the insanity of herring fishing but was looking forward to it.
He was bright and amiable, as was Karl, making me immediately
feel silly for all the anxiety I'd felt on the drive down. But there was
good reason for it, dating back to that first trip on the *Lancer*.

• • •

In the afternoon, after a break for lunch, we crew members set off
together to run last minute errands. It was a group effort, shop-
ping, roving the aisles, looking for anything and everything, from
fruit to cookies, to enormous, bulk-food boxes of Cheez-Its—
Karl's sworn remedy for the settling of stomachs on the roughest
seas—absolutely anything we might crave and that might make our
journey and our confinement over the next six to eight weeks as
comfortable as possible.

"I always dread taking off when I'm sitting at home," said Karl
at one point, "but once we start gearing up and getting ready I can't
help but get excited." He had become more animated than I'd ever
seen him in the coffee shop. There, he was so much more formal—
especially when his wife and kids were with him—not really "one
of the guys."

But the camaraderie and the anticipation had begun to build
in all of us, especially Brad, who would be heading north for the

first time. "I can't wait to get out and see the coast," he exclaimed more than once. His enthusiasm was infectious, and my nerves were now completely quelled, replaced by this sudden bond—this compatibility and easy-going anticipation; it almost felt as if we were buddies preparing for a camping trip, which made all the work flow that much smoother.

However, I was caught a bit off guard when at the last minute we ducked into the liquor store. Most of the boats I'd worked on had been dry—no alcohol. My surprise must have registered.

"Tim's okay with it," Karl immediately explained. "As long as we keep it low key, and it's only when we're anchored up someplace calm after the work's done."

"And you're only allowed one," added Brad, though Karl gave him a look like that rule might be bent occasionally. "No, really," Brad continued. "Tim's pretty strict about that."

"As long as you don't get caught," said Karl, with a mischievous-ness that seemed out of character.

Not sure what to say, I shrugged it off and pitched in some money for beer and a couple of bottles of whiskey. Though I was as likely to tip a few as the next guy, I'd seen enough to know how quickly it could all turn around out there, even in calm water, and I certainly didn't want to have to rely on anyone under the influence.

Karl must have sensed my concern. "No worries," he said. "We're pretty careful. Tim's probably one of the most safety-conscious skip-pers out there."

He was right. There had been a big push by the Coast Guard and commercial fishing groups to make the industry safer, but Tim had other reasons to take it seriously.

The next morning I saw firsthand just how seriously Tim took safety when he gathered his crew around the galley table for a briefing followed by a walk-through drill. Tim was a big guy, balding, with a full, wide face, not tall but somewhat stout and, at least on the exterior, completely sure of himself—which a skipper should be if they are going to run a boat. It's a trait you want to see in your captain, someone who is confident in their abilities but not cocky. He was good natured and easygoing, but resolute as he listed where we each needed to go and what our duties would be if a man fell overboard, if there was a fire, or if the boat was going down. We discussed how to deploy the life raft, who would grab the EPIRB—the Emergency Position Indicating Radio Beacon that automatically signals the Coast Guard—and when to don our bright orange survival suits. Bulky, buoyant, and insulating, these full-body "Gumby suits," while nearly impossible to move around in on land will keep you floating and alive in the water for many hours—hopefully long enough to be rescued. We even took them out to wax the zippers, and for kicks tested just how fast we could crawl into them, the goal being under a minute. It was good to go through these precautions, but we all hoped we'd never have to put any of them into effect.

• • •

Compared to my early days as a fisherman, things were really kind of low-key on the *Iliamna Bay*, and not just because I knew how to tie a knot and stack a seine. It went deeper than that, a connection I'd developed to the sea, perhaps, and to these guys—even though we'd just met. Seining is like being part of a team, the way you have to work fast and in unison, anticipating your teammates' moves when you lay out the gear, even the way tasks are delegated, the skipper controlling the flow, sometimes barking orders like a coach.

We all felt like this was a good fit, that we would work well together. It was obvious in the free flow of conversation as we went about menial tasks, passing the time with stories of how we'd arrived at this point, finding ourselves here on the deck of an Alaskan fishing boat. So as is often the case with fishermen, happenstance had landed us here, and once again I was astonished at the strange course life sometimes takes and how serendipity often dictates where we go and where we end up. In this instance, Karl and I had been steered on such similar paths, albeit his had begun a bit earlier. Karl and I had grown up not far from one another in upstate New York and had each made our way north between semesters at nearby campuses.

"It was really weird," said Karl, explaining the circumstances of how he first arrived in Alaska. "I'd flown into Anchorage with a friend from school and we just started hitchhiking, not sure where we were going. Some guy does a U-turn, crossing traffic, going out of his way to pick us up. I guess he wants some company, says he's going to Homer, suggests we go, and he even gets us a job on the slime line at the old Whitney-Fidalgo plant. Then, not long after that we strike up a conversation with this random guy and he happens to be from Plattsburgh, my home town. Out of all these people hanging around he happens to know my family and is good friends with my older brother, and he takes us to Clam Gulch and gets us on with the Osmars, setnetting."

"Funny how things happen," I said. "With me it was a guy at the Buffalo Folk Festival. A buddy and I were planning to take off as soon as school was finished for the year, and out of thirty thousand people at the concert, who should we sit next to but my buddy's long-lost childhood friend who happens to work every summer in the cannery in Seward. So that's where we were going."

As it turned out, we had both worked summers before moving north for good, imported our girlfriends from New York, fished and worked odd jobs, before eventually finding ourselves here together on the deck of the *Iliamna Bay*. And now we were preparing for an adventure that would not only continue our journeys, but would be a defining moment in our intersecting lives.

4

ALASKA OR BUST

SEWARD, MAY 1984

IT WAS SIX thousand hard miles on an already tired Ford Granada—
a poor old car not really known for its dependability and loaded
to the hilt: roof rack piled high with tents and camping gear, trunk
crammed with food, sleeping bags, and spare clothing, day packs at
our feet, boombox shuffled from one lap to the next. The Granada
was sitting so low that as it passed the notorious hump at the end
of the driveway, a scraping like a tremendous shiver rose through
our feet. Yet accompanying it was an immense feeling of abandon
and freedom at finally being underway, plunging headlong into that
great series of asphalt rivers, their current to carry us north out of
New York and into Canada, and then for the next two weeks west,
into the unknown.

It was early May, and with me for the very beginning of the
summer travel season was Moo, an incessant talker from New York
City, and his guitar-picking buddy Dave, and Dave's girlfriend Peggy.
Together we took our place in a long procession of cars, trucks, and
travel trailers. We watched as their fumes and dust rose up in a
sun-soaked cloud, waiting our turn for the border guard to finally
bend down and inspect our car, loaded so top-heavy it looked as
if it might topple over at any moment. It was difficult not to feel
a bit suspect as he took an interest in us, glancing with a scant
smile over the front of the car and commenting on the cockeyed

piece of screen fastened over the grill and headlights—a precaution somebody had told us about to protect the car from flying debris. I looked around too at this point, at the array of other vehicles next to and behind us, suddenly feeling conspicuous and out of place among the vacationers, salesmen, and truckers. We didn't look like any of them. We were the Joad family turned hippy, heading to Alaska rather than California, to salmon rather than grapes—with the same high expectation though hopefully with far better results.

It was nearly a week before we reached the Al-Can, the Alaska-Canada Highway; in those days it was mostly a dirt and gravel artery built hastily by soldiers during World War II. It was infamous for its clouds of swirling dust; when it rained, they would settle into potholes of thick gravy—booby traps lying in wait for unsuspecting cars.

By the time we reached the Al-Can's start in British Columbia we were just about out of money. A series of minor repairs along with overpriced gas, food, and beer, had sucked up just about our last penny and overshadowed any excitement we might have had when we finally crossed into Alaska several days later.

To make matters worse it had begun to rain. And this was nothing like the New York summer rains I was used to: rain that came in a giant cloudburst, triggered by and quelling an oppressive shroud of humidity, the sun quickly returning to steam you warm and dry. No, this was dark, cold, and insidious and came in a siege of downpours followed by a series of slow, penetrating mists—mists that seemed to sneak up and never leave.

Due to our rather dire financial quandary, we decided not to linger. We would forego any sightseeing and shoot straight for Seward, across a state one-third the size of the Lower 48. That's when I realized just how big Alaska actually was. It took the better part of the next afternoon and all night to reach our destination.

Completely worn out by hours of endless driving, a sea of bad coffee, and the nagging thought of our now empty coffers, I was left wondering what we'd do for even basic necessities. And the rain showed no signs of letting up, continuing in varying degrees for the next four days. As far as I could tell there was nothing more to Alaska than one immense fog bank interspersed with sheets of rain. This picture I had so longed to see was no more than a drab canvas of brown and gray. Even sleep was restless and came only in short intervals, between which I tried to ignore the drumbeat of implied disaster as it pounded on the outside of my tent. Fortunately we hadn't come across any newspapers on our way south from Anchorage. If we had, we would have learned that two nights before in our campground—perhaps in our very spot—there had been a double homicide . . . over a case of beer.

During this time we had no choice but to walk everywhere because there was no money left for gas. We hiked first to the cannery, a ghost town of pea-green steel buildings that looked as though they had been hurriedly erected sometime during the previous century. An ominous pall was cast over the entire complex where we had hoped to work; it was completely devoid of people, locked up tight, and shrouded in that perpetual mist.

After our disappointing stop at the cannery, where it didn't look like anyone would be working for quite some time, we made our way along a road that followed the shoreline of something that seemed very large. We couldn't see it but could sense it—could smell its size on the breeze, taste it in that heavy, oyster-shell air that follows low tide. It was Resurrection Bay, lost in the fog somewhere to the right of us. When we ran out of road, we circled back along the main drag, lined with yet-to-open gift shops and tourist traps, lively taverns we couldn't afford, and a homestyle café that touted a magnificent-smelling breakfast, which was priced more than three-times what it would have cost back in New York.

So instead we spent the very last of our money on peanut butter and dry cereal, and in order to stay out of the rain we ate in the car. We hoofed it three miles to the local public library. Despite its sign at the front desk—CANNERY WORKERS: NO FISH CLOTHES. NO NAPPING. THE LIBRARY IS FOR READING—we hung out there for hours on end because it was the only free dry place in town.

Then, sometime during my fifth night in Seward, the interminable drumming of the rain finally ceased. Having grown so used to it, the lack of sound and its accompanying chill seemed somehow incongruous—especially come morning when I awoke to an unfamiliar brightness, to a tent damp not with rain but with condensation and transformed into a sweltering canvas oven. Dressing quickly, I emerged into a changed world. The enormous spruce trees were steaming between shadows broken by a blindingly bright light. Drops of dew clung to their branches, outlined in the forgotten bounty of the sun.

Shielding my eyes, I made my way to the edge of our campground, not sure exactly what to expect. There was something dramatic in the offing, more than the weather simply having changed. It was impossible to pinpoint until I reached the edge of the campground, where the trees stood aside and where, up a small knoll and next to a narrow dirt road, something completely new unfolded before me: a fresh portrait of Alaska. Suddenly unveiled in front of me, it far surpassed even my most romantic of notions.

5

SPIT RAT

ILIAMNA BAY, APRIL 1997

ALMOST INSTANTANEOUSLY, THE minute Karl discovered we both came from upstate New York, he began telling me his story as we worked. While Karl's introduction to the Last Frontier may have been more gracious than mine it was no less immediate. "I still had some money," he said, "and got a job right away, but I was just as taken by all of this." There was a resonance in his voice as he fanned his arm across the deck and paused to look around. It was as if he had opened a curtain to reveal a vast panorama—360 degrees of natural wonder that had surrounded us all this time but that we had taken for granted as we worked.

"How could you not be?" I said, stopping to share his reverence, the mountains primordial and windswept, reminding me once again why I was here and here to stay, and once again heading out to sea.

"It was a great time, too," Karl recalled. "Not a care in the world back then."

"I guess so." I wasn't entirely sure I agreed with him. I could still remember what it was like to be broke and on my own for the first time. I imagined Karl in the village of Homer; with its more artsy vibe and reputation as Alaska's most left-leaning stronghold, even back then it was probably much more accepting of a longhaired college kid trying to find himself. For starters, there wouldn't have been a rude sign in the Homer library. And there was the "Homer spit." It is an elongated finger of rock and sand, and a major feature in the geography of the area, jutting for miles into the sea and helping to form Kachemak Bay. It was where our boat was now tied, and it had long been a Mecca for the wayward vagabond. Back in the day there were fewer tourist shops and restaurants.When Karl arrived this now valuable piece of real estate would have been full of fish buying stations and cold-storage production lines instead. It was before the hotels and fancy boutiques had taken over, before the city decided to crack down on freeloaders, slimers, and wannabe fishermen—all the colorful inhabitants once known as "spit rats," of which Karl had been one.

"There were a bunch of us. Oddballs, for sure," admitted Karl, looking back with both fondness and appreciation. "But a lot of good people, too," he added. "It was funny, they were living all over the place, in everything from old retorts to pallet houses—regular Taj Mahals made out of driftwood and blue tarps. And everybody seemed to get along. Sometimes we'd all get together, the whole spit, and if not you'd make your way from campfire to campfire, meeting everybody. I'm even still in touch with some of those folks."

6

SECOND THOUGHTS AND SECOND CHANCES

SEWARD, MAY 1984

IN SEWARD, WE didn't have it so easy. There was no central gathering place. Instead, coveys of campers and elaborate little tent villages were tucked into the woods or stationed on someone's spare lot. The people who lived in these were mostly old timers returning for their second or third season at the cannery or getting ready to board a boat. The rest of us—the newbies—gathered in the public campgrounds, which, back then, were still free. Though just about every open space in our campground, Forest Acres, was dotted with a tent, during the rains I had rarely come across any inhabitants—only an occasional shadow scurrying to the outhouse, dodging raindrops and nodding a brief, downtrodden hello. But once the sun finally appeared and looked as though it were going to stay awhile, everyone came out like forest nymphs emerging after a long hibernation. Free from their nylon hovels, they were as giddy as I was and as anxious for conversation and companionship.

There were all kinds, and in the same haggard condition. They were cold, wet, and in the most uncertain of financial quandaries— yet all at once full of the expectation and promise of Alaska. The fates had landed us here, and for no reason other than that our tents were pitched nearby, we came together.

There was a pair of eighteen-year-olds, fresh out of high school, whom we had met back in British Columbia. There was a Vietnam veteran named Alan, who perhaps had spent too many nights on the jungle floor, because he refused to sleep on the ground. Instead, he chose to pitch his tent rather precariously upon the hard face of a picnic table. And there was a couple with quite an obvious age-difference between them: Mark was his late twenties, Faye in her early fifties. They had made the trip all the way from Texas in a car much older and more decrepit than mine and they shared a notice-ably small, hurriedly obtained pup tent that looked hardly capable of shedding the rain and often perilously close to blowing away.

While this group staked its claim to a corner of the campground and waited for the season to begin, a multitude of names and faces passed before the flames of our evening fire. Over the next few weeks college students, unemployed factory workers, world trav-elers, and even a few PhDs, from everywhere across the country, came drifting by hoping to find adventure and work aboard the boats or at the cannery. The cannery, we learned, would not open for nearly another month. Upon hearing this, many moved on.

Those of us who decided to stay and wait out the month—most because we had no money to move on with—pitched in every eve-ning for a communal hoboes' feast.

Although signs warned of prosecution to the fullest extent of the law, we occasionally poached a sockeye (or red salmon), out of a nearby creek. All we ever took was one or two at a time, but it was enough—along with whatever we stuffed it with—to feed the entire group. We even used the inedible parts as bait for rockfish, which could be caught at high tide on a beach on the outskirts of town. Often, if not a meal in itself, the rockfish would serve as the main ingredient, along with bread and fiddlehead ferns in our stuffing.

We'd also pass the hat around to visitors and campground residents alike, pooling what little spare change we had for the cheapest of the cheap local brew. Then we would stay up late and marvel at the midnight sun, a spectacle most of us, having never ventured so far north, could hardly fathom. Its intoxicating presence made sleep impossible as we continued into the early morning hours sharing stories and trading lies around the fading embers of the night's campfire.

Each morning was a race to the state employment center, where everyone hoped to be first in line for day labor. This usually entailed doing yard work at one of Seward's more respectable residences—forty, maybe fifty bucks that felt like a million. Or if you were really lucky, perhaps a multi-day job scraping barnacles and old paint off a boat in dry dock.

This is when I really got to know Mark. We tended to team up on day labor, including the painting of a house, which lasted the better part of a week, with the added bonus of lunch breaks, the owner of the house treating us to a meal of anything we wanted at the restaurant of our choice.

As we headed to this and other jobs in Mark's car I would glance over at him sitting beside me. He was so different than me, twenty-nine or thirty years to my twenty and stocky, with a thick head of dark blond hair, beneath which the dreams churned away as his fingers clenched into tight fists on the steering wheel, letters tattooed on each—L-O-V-E on one hand, H-A-T-E on the other. There was something about him—a danger, yes, but a certain confidence that I, having spent most of my short life in school, had not seen very much of. It wasn't the confidence you gain on the football field or in the lecture hall. It was the confidence you get nowhere else but on the street, a gritty self-assuredness that says "don't fuck with me," and I liked being a part of it, near it, next to it. "We're not going to mess with you," it said, "but by God, you better leave us the hell alone."

When we weren't working we sat—sometimes for hours—at the employment center. As we did, the people who worked there would continually feed us the same warning: that all we had heard was not true, that jobs in Alaska were not plentiful, did not pay much, and contrary to what we'd been told by those who already worked at the cannery, were not very easy to get.

Every time I entered the sterile confines of the state office building and took my place on the hard bench in the anterior office, the dread would re-emerge. It would grow as I shook off the remnants of the short night and once again became aware of the lingering odor of wood smoke and spilled beer permeating my now old and hopelessly stained clothes.

But it was a dread that was also short-lived, forgotten the minute we were called upon for a job, or if no work was available, when we were set free to explore, spending the afternoon happily crawling down steep canyons in order to comb a secluded stretch of favorite beach, or wrestling our way through thickets of alder and prickly devil's club in order to find a perch among the ancient peaks. It was on these vistas, on the edge of the world, where the reigning backdrop of the Gulf of Alaska takes precedence, that the tiny problems of town and money were rendered insignificant.

Then, each night, we would return to our campsite both exhausted and exalted after a day of working or hiking, returning to this group and the fellowship of poverty and hope that bound us together.

And together it was we would finally, after nearly six weeks, trudge to the cannery orientation, or *pre*-orientation really, to let us see what we were in for, what we were up against, *if* we were even hired.

Will you stick it out? Do you have what it takes?—that's what the young manager seemed to be asking. Could we hack working here, in so dank and dark a facility and surrounded by such loud and incredibly dangerous machinery, machinery that looked as though it had materialized out of the dawning of the industrial revolution? Was this the place we really wanted to spend the best part of our summer, where the adventure wears off after a few minutes of standing in the same spot, up to our ankles in cold fish guts, part of a somnambulistic army in constant battle with boredom, cleaning the same belly of a different fish over and over and over again, for twelve, thirteen, fourteen hours a day? It was almost as if they were trying to talk us out of, not into, working there.

"But that," said the cannery spokesman, point-blank, "is the whole reason for this pre-orientation: to save us from hiring people who can't hack it."

Unfortunately, what this young man and his company did not understand was that poverty makes people think they can do anything. And there were fifty of us at this—the first of three pre-orientations—who not only thought we could hack it, but were enthusiastic at the prospect.

"Believe it or not," the young man warned, "by the end of the summer only about thirty percent of you—if you're hired—will still be around. And only about half of that number will return the following summer."

Yet none of us seemed convinced. Except Mark, that was.

"That cannery's not for me," he said around the campfire that evening, his quiet face punctuated by the scars of a life much different from mine. "I know what it's like," he went on. "I spent two years at a meat packing plant—a showroom compared to this cannery. And let me tell you, it was awful."

That's when he first mentioned fishing. "I used to work on a shrimper," he said. "It's great. You're not working for some big company." It sounded as if he was trying to convince me of something. He looked straight at me. "Hell, you're outside where there's lots of elbow room, lots of room for a man to breathe . . . and you get to see some of this country. I'm going to make this my home and I want to see as much of it as I can. Yup, I'm going to work on a boat. I've been hittin' the docks and got a few leads."

Despite the stories of tremendous catches and deckhands scoring huge sums of money that were continually circulating, until then I hadn't seriously considered fishing. No, I'd take my chances at the cannery. Besides, after nearly a month, the campground was beginning to feel like home and those sharing it a family—albeit an odd and very extended family to be sure.

No more was said about fishing or about boats, and nearly a week later, with the opening of salmon season right around the corner, everything began to change. The pace around town, on the docks, at the cannery, even in the campground, had picked up tenfold and the energy was palpable. And with that sudden surge of activity, I had my interview and was hired on at the cannery along with most of my friends. All were ecstatic and utterly relieved. It was always a party around the fire at night, but now there was reason for cheer. For the first time since arriving, I actually felt as if everything might work out.

7

A GREAT OPPORTUNITY

IN ANTICIPATION OF work many had gone off to do chores, heading to the Laundromat or buying supplies for lunches, or anything else they thought they might need at the cannery. I was enjoying a quiet, leisurely afternoon at the campground, likely my last for a long while. That's about the time Mark came charging around the corner, a wake of dust rising behind his old car as he screeched to a halt in front of our little encampment. He had another guy with him, a silent character with a tired face and one of those ancient seafarer's beards—a beard like the one Gregory Peck sported in the movie version of *Moby Dick,* one that crawls around the chin but stays clear of the upper lip.

"Hey, just the guy I was lookin' for," he said with a big grin. "Got a job on one of those boats I was tellin' you about. They need another hand. You interested?"

I wasn't sure what to say. Most of those stories about big money were probably exaggerated, but if I'd learned anything during my short stay in Alaska it's that it's much better to be a fisherman than a cannery worker. It's a much higher station in life. If you're lucky enough to work on one of the better boats—one of those highliners, the boats that bring in the top catches—it can even border on eminence. Some of the richest people in the state were highliners. But Mark must have sensed my hesitation.

"You don't want to work at that cannery," he said. "Inside all summer, workin' for slave wages. You'll make some real money on this boat. This guys been fishin' a long time." I assumed he was talking about the guy standing there with him, who still had not said a word.

"I don't know," I mumbled.

"What do you mean, you don't know? This is a great opportunity and it's being handed right to you. We're leaving tomorrow. Come meet Woody."

"Woody?" I asked.

"The skipper," said Mark. "Of the *Lancer*." As if this was information I somehow ought to know.

"Oh yeah," I said, "right." If Woody was the skipper, who was this other guy, this quiet man? I wasn't anywhere near this boat— what was it, the *Lancer*?—and already I was confused. I wondered to myself, how could I even consider such a thing, bypassing what was obvious and easy? It was an opportunity all right—to be in an extreme situation, someplace completely uncomfortable, and away from my friends. But isn't that what made it a genuine adventure, isn't that what brought me to Alaska in the first place?

"Well," asked Mark. "I wouldn't pass this up if I were you, it's a great opportunity."

8

GEARING UP

ILIAMNA BAY, APRIL 1997

I COULD SEE AS we bundled up our extra seine, to be handed over to the cannery and shipped west on a tender, that Karl was a natural born teacher. "Let's do it this way," he'd suggest, or he might say, "That's the way I think Tim wants it done." It would be easy to piss off a fellow deckhand by telling them what to do, but Karl, who was actually considering returning to school to pursue elementary education, knew enough about the sea, about people, and about this particular boat, to share his knowledge in a way that was completely understandable and not condescending in the least.

Brad, who had graduated from college not long ago and was planning a career in audio engineering, would officially be cook, though he made it clear that the rest of us were free to join in anytime. He had organized the kitchen and gave us a tour, so we'd know where to find something between meals. Tim, who was common-sense shrewd and experienced, gave last-minute instructions on equipment and minimal lessons on keeping the engine running throughout the night, so we would not have to wake him up while we were on wheel watch—driving the boat to our next opening, which, in the case of Bristol Bay, was five or six days, and nights, of constant travel.

We'd take watches at two-hour intervals, Tim informed us. "If you feel like going longer that's fine," he said. "I just don't want anyone falling asleep."

If it was nighttime, I knew what that meant; for most of us at least, it meant ending our watch as soon as it was over. Sure, there were some guys who thrived on the danger and didn't seem to care that they had nearly a million dollars worth of boat—not to mention the lives of their crewmates—in their hands. But if it was dark, pitch black, and we were navigating on radar and GPS, and especially if it was stormy and the boat was pitching and rolling, most of us were thankful the minute the two-hour mark was up. If, however, some-one's watch fell at sunrise and the winds were relatively calm, with Dall porpoise riding in the boat's wake, perhaps a whale spouting on the horizon, flocks of seagulls merrily announcing the oncoming day—that's when most of us would stay at our post and marvel at how lucky we were. How there was no place on Earth we'd rather be. It was to be savored, because we all knew that without even a moment's notice it could all change—anything could cause disaster, from a mechanical problem to the next storm, and we had to be ready. And I was sure we were.

Gearing up was quickly done. Still, we'd wait a night before shoving off, just to catch our breath and to have one last evening on shore—Tim and Karl with their families, Brad and I sharing a few beers in town. In the morning there would be time over a lei-surely breakfast to re-evaluate the situation and think about any-thing we might have overlooked. With Tim's attention for detail I doubted there'd be much left to do. Our larders were full, gear ready. Morning would come quickly, and soon we'd be underway.

9

SO YOU WANT TO BE
A FISHERMAN?

LANCER, JUNE 1984

WHO, IN THEIR earliest twenties could be anything but unsure of themselves, yet so much less cautious about taking a chance? That was me: new to Alaska, wide-eyed, and willing to go anywhere life took me. So it was with barely a hesitation that I climbed into the car with Mark and The Quiet Man, and in a cloud of dust we took off toward the Seward boat harbor.

If I'd known anything whatsoever about the sea, about fishing, or about boats, the fact that the *Lancer* needed two deckhands—two *greenhorn* deckhands—just days before the season opened would have tipped me off and would have sent a bright red flare above the turbid sea of my brain, warning me of impending disaster. But I didn't know the first thing about the sea, this boat, or about Mark, for that matter, and no warning flare was ever lit.

On our way to the harbor we passed the vast, rusty array of blue and green cannery buildings, a corroded, self-contained village that had suddenly come to life with forklifts, cranes, and a flotilla of boats gearing up for the approaching season. Following a quaint seaside street dotted with small gift shops, tour operators, and charter fishing outfits, we passed boats held suspended in dry dock, perched high on rusty barrels and 2x4s. These were either being diligently worked—sanded, caulked, and painted in a frenzy—or sitting neglected, dilapidated, and repossessed. The smell of dreams filled the air, those of fiberglass and fresh paint mixing with the dry rot of those long forgotten. The ghosts of each passing season hanging on the breeze, waiting to be caught and resurrected by newcomers like us.

I looked at Mark sitting there. Though he had the air of a rough older brother, he could be, at the same time, trusting and somehow childlike. One minute a man of the world, the next asking me for something I thought everyone knew, like helping him mail a package or make a transaction at the bank. Either way, as we emerged from the car and headed to the docks, I was glad he was there, glad he'd be with me on this first giant leap into the unknown.

The Quiet Man took the lead, down a ramp and into the world of boats. I had no idea there could be so many. We walked past all kinds, sail and power boats owned mostly by businesspeople from the suburbs of Anchorage who would drive down for a weekend during summer to polish their teak and sip martinis on the back decks. Perhaps they'd take their friends on a little trip around the bay or an occasional troll for salmon. Then we passed the tour and charter boats: large hundred-foot vessels, windowed water buses, fiberglass and utilitarian, their lines straight and not very pretty; or twenty-five-foot aluminum-hulled speedsters set up for sport, halibut poles racked up like weaponry along the outside of their cabin walls.

We headed on to where the working boats were tied, a flurry of activity crossing each slip—men and a few women, tough looking and road-weary, coiling lines, stacking and mending nets, scraping last minute paint and putty. I knew immediately these men and women lived much nearer to Mark's world than mine; they all appeared to possess at least some of that same swagger, something I hoped might rub off on me.

"Hey, you guys got everything ready to go?" someone called from the deck of one of the boats.

"Yeah, you bet," The Quiet Man called back, acknowledging a fellow sea dog with the first of his few words and a wave of his hand. He was clearly a part of the annual hustle and drive that springs to life on the docks each year—fishermen and boat people emerging from the winter woodwork. The good ones and the lucky ones, who caught a lot of fish last year, returning from months on a beach in the South Pacific or Central America; those not so lucky, the sourdoughs—sour because they're stuck in Alaska, with no dough to get out—back from a hard winter spent in the local bars or under the harsh city lights of Anchorage. Whether tanned and trim and full of sun and surf, or down and out and full of drink and despair, they all knew The Quiet Man who walked among the docks in every port town, as much a part of the annual transitory realm of the sea as the tides. It was a realm I saw through a landlubber's eyes, rough, dirty, and untamed . . . and so unmistakably foreign.

Too far in to turn back now, I followed Mark and The Quiet Man deeper into uncharted territory, finally rounding the corner onto another finger of dock and ambling down a long row of vessels before spotting the one we were after. It's name, *Lancer*, was not written in some fancy Gothic script, like many of the boats we'd passed, or in carefully painted block letters, but stenciled haphazardly across its bow, the way the letters were scrawled on Mark's fingers, as an afterthought or just another job to do.

That's when I saw Woody on deck, old and weather-worn and engrossed in the intricate task of splicing two pieces of line into one. The old man looked a lot like the *Lancer*—compact, tempered, yet battered and a bit rusty. Perhaps he'd been one of those spending a long winter in the bars of Seward.

He looked up as we approached, absently dropping the ball of line that had so absorbed him a moment earlier. He wore a sort of spotted, chocolate-brown cap that once must have been as white as his remaining hair but was now stained with what looked like years of diesel oil and grease. I couldn't help but notice his hands; they were squat and leathery like a pair of old-time baseball mitts that hadn't been oiled in decades and shy a few fingers.

"Woody," Mark said, surprising me how sheepish his voice suddenly sounded, "this is my friend—the one I was telling you about."

Something about the way he sized me up from the deck of his boat, his stance, his stabbing glare—a look that told me he and he alone was the boss, off shore and on—made me hesitate, even when he finally asked us in a gravelly voice to come aboard. But as we began to take that step over the rail and onto the boat he stopped short, turning abruptly to look me in the eye and catching just a glint of my momentary panic.

"So, you want to be a fisherman," he said, more of a wager than a question.

Then, without waiting for a response he quickly turned, leading us into his kingdom, the beginning of my long and desultory alternative education. My introduction to the sea.

10

CONFIDENCE AND NERVE

NOT KNOWING ENOUGH to even word an intelligent question I let Mark and Woody do most of the talking. I just sat there and listened as Mark asked about the type of fishing we'd be doing—purse seining. This was new to Mark as well, although he professed to having worked on various shrimpers in the Gulf of Mexico.

I understood from the conversation that this boat required a four member crew, which would consist of myself, Mark, The Quiet Man, and Woody. I learned that one end of the net, or seine, would be attached to the skiff, the other end to the *Lancer*. Along the top of the net ran the cork line, a thick floating line with corks spaced every couple of feet for buoyancy; along the bottom was the heavy lead line, which would sink. The idea was to encircle a school of salmon with this huge net. The net would then be placed over the giant mechanical pulley—called a block—that was suspended from the boom of the boat. Corks, lead line, and web would be stacked on deck until the circle of net was small enough to purse— a method of bringing the lead line up under the fish, closing them off, and trapping them in the "purse" of net.

It wasn't much to go on, and as far as instruction it was apparent my teacher was not the nurturing type. After forty years of fishing and forty years of hard living and equally hard drinking, and after what sounded like several marriages, old Woody conjured up thoughts of Jack London's *The Sea Wolf*. A Wolf Larsen to my

Humphrey van Weyden; I immediately brushed the notion aside, but time and again over the course of our voyage it would fall startlingly to mind.

"So, Mark tells me you have some experience on boats." He finally addressed me.

"Well," I stumbled. "I guess."

"You guess?"

"I have some," I blurted out. "On small boats, skiffs. On lakes mostly. I don't get seasick." At least I didn't think so.

"That's good," grunted the old man. "No commercial experience, though?"

"No," I fessed up. "Afraid not."

"Well, everybody's got to learn sometime," said Woody without so much as a smile and once again looking me up and down. "I've sure broken in my share of deckhands over the years."

"Broken in? You mean broken, don't you, Woody?" The Quiet Man had stuck his head inside the cabin door and to my surprise, put together a complete sentence. A joke at that.

Woody nodded in agreement, a knowing grin finally breaking the stiff contours of his face. "Yeah, I've broken my share, too," he said, before sending us away and warning that we'd better be back ready for work early in the morning.

Something should have tipped me off. I should have known, then and there, what I was getting in to. Hell, I'd only seen the ocean a couple times. Frankly, I had no business even being on a boat. And when Woody gazed at me with that severe and demanding look, it should have served as a warning, an invitation to stay put on friendly ground, my last chance to take the slow grind of the cannery over the quick, turbulent impulse of the sea and the men who lived by it.

But I had no way of knowing then the enormous difference between confidence and nerve; that you can be confident in your own ability, for instance, yet terribly afraid at the same time. And back then, while confidence may have been in short supply, nerve was something I had plenty of. And because of that nerve, and because Woody had let us go for the night and we were walking away, free until the next morning—an eternity—any reluctance vanished. Because the smell of the ocean was so consuming, because I was suddenly inexplicably intoxicated by the thrill of this new world and the mystery of the unknown, I simply chose to ignore any warning. I simply went merrily along my way, actually living for the moment, following Mark blindly back to the campground, and tomorrow following him into the abyss.

• • •

That night, as the campground dined on shrimp and rockfish, Mark foresaw a future that was hardy and prosperous, making a living as men of the past had done: fishing throughout the summer, prospecting for gold in the fall, and learning to trap in the winter. He rarely talked about the past. The only time he'd mentioned some family, a father and a couple of siblings, was to say they were "no good," and that he didn't really care if he saw them again. Faye on the other hand, who had been working in a convenience store when she met Mark, seemed more forthcoming. She had been married for a long time and had grown bored. She also often talked about her adult children, who she missed. It might have been why she tended to mother the rest of us—many of us likely younger than her own kids.

Mark went on to predict a modest, hard-working, yet comfortable life in a cabin he would build himself on the shore of a lake somewhere. A new beginning for him and Faye. It was nice to hear him talk and dream, speculating on the small fortune he assured me we'd make that summer, as I sat beside him fumbling with a couple of scraps of spare line. Woody had handed them to Mark as we left. "You better practice your knots," Woody had said. "Bowline, half hitch, clove hitch. And you better learn your friend some, too. He's going to need them."

I practiced well into the night, though my attempts to tie the knots grew more troublesome the later it got. With each beer and then several shots of some rotgut whiskey, they became impossible and finally I gave up. I would practice more at dawn, I assured myself.

• • •

I got up early despite all we had to drink—the morning upon me much sooner than expected. I made sure I had packed all my warmest clothes—sweatshirts, sweaters, long johns. I also packed a bulky winter parka, which for some reason would turn out to be an instant source of derision on the *Lancer*, but would allow me my brief, necessary respites on deck, away from the others.

Then I went for a walk and looked around. There were dark clouds on the horizon, toward the sea, for the first time in about three weeks. And an early morning breeze was on the rise. It seemed odd. Even back when it was raining every day the mornings had been without wind, and I wondered what this change signified.

11

SETTING SAIL

ILIAMNA BAY, APRIL 1997

THOUGH THE *Iliamna Bay* was fueled and ready, we took our time, making sure once again that the skiff was firmly chained on deck and that we hadn't forgotten anything. The most dangerous situations usually occur during transit, rather than on the fishing grounds or anchored somewhere. That's often when you encounter trouble—an engine malfunction or fire, something tearing loose on deck, a careless crewman falling overboard—and it usually occurs when the weather is at its most horrific and help a long way off. We'd all heard the stories, perhaps even had some of our own, of seas so severe they smashed the plexiglass windows out of wheelhouses, of rogue waves that came out of nowhere and sent the largest, most seaworthy boats careening down a mountain of water. And to some degree we had each experienced weather so bad you were begging for it to be over, wishing you could be anywhere else. And worst of all, in times like these everything languishes, especially your progress. Time seems to drive to a standstill—and usually in direct proportion to your growing fear and anxiety—especially when forced to alter your course and in the worst case having to heave-to into extreme weather. It may keep your boat in one piece, but it also prolongs the agony.

But when we untied at midmorning and made our way out of the harbor, you couldn't have asked for a finer day. The seas were calm, streaks of sun breaking through the bank of distant cumulus clouds. Almost immediately, that nagging pre-trip anticipation abated and any sadness at leaving—even the slightest trace of regret—dissipated. It never failed—the minute we left the dock and began to feel the roll of the waves, the salt-sea air intermingling with a slight taste of diesel, and it's as if I were instantly transported into the here and now and all was as it should be: amazing and beautiful. There was nothing except the voyage ahead.

We all settled in for the trip across Cook Inlet, to the herring grounds of Kamishak Bay. With a running speed of only seven to eight nautical miles or knots an hour, it would be an all-day affair. We would likely be dropping the pick, or anchor, sometime around sunset—about nine o' clock this time of year—trying to hold tight in one of the worst anchorages we knew of, behind Mount Augustine, a currently dormant island volcano.

When I'd headed out of Homer on previous trips, it was usually in a southerly direction, around the outer edge of the Kenai Peninsula and then into the vastness of the Gulf of Alaska and toward Prince William Sound. But with the *Exxon Valdez* oil spill eight years earlier, the herring population, along with their price, had plummeted. Of course, company officials denied any part in the demise of Prince William Sound's herring, no matter that the spill occurred during the peak of spawning season.

But on this trip, we would head northwest out of Homer, and I would miss the ethereal beauty of the outer coast. Despite the fickle weather, there's something essential and raw, something invigorating, in the outer coast's power and energy—the way the ocean crashes upon those steep, inhospitable cliffs. Inhospitable for humans, that is. In truth, you don't have to look very far to see that these sheer, desperate outcroppings are filled with life. A cacophonous variety of birds perch and nest on the cliffs, and if you look carefully, mountain goats cling to a fragile existence on the highest precipices.

I would also miss reaching the sound, navigating around the lush islands marking its entrance, and coming to rest in a much more suitable anchorage. While Kamishak Bay has its own allure, early in the year it is a stark, barren landscape, and behind Augustine Island lies that notoriously bad anchorage that none of us were looking forward to.

On the bright side, this made for a shorter trip. And that suited us just fine, as it took a good portion of the crossing to even begin to accustom ourselves to the vibration and continuous drone of the motor, which was further accentuated by the size and age of our vessel. With earplugs constantly in use, conversation was necessarily held to a minimum. Fortunately, Karl had come prepared with books of number and word games, like Sudoko and word searches, but mostly crossword puzzles culled from the previous month's newspapers. With the eternal rumble of the engine, talk gave way to pointing, okay signs, even the occasional one finger salute, with actual dialogue quickly dissolving into thought.

Brad had made cookies before we left, and he kept a pot of chili warm on the galley's kerosene stove, there for the taking whenever we were hungry or just bored. On a long voyage, we were almost always bored. It's no wonder that so many professional tendermen—the crew of the boats that not only tender herring in April and May but go on to follow the salmon fleet all summer throughout the state—end up so large. By the end of the season, some are barely even able to squeeze through the galley doors.

I was working aboard a tender one year when a football game was suggested among the crews of several of the anchored boats. Looking at these large, visually menacing skippers and deckhands, I was skeptical about joining. And when it was ruled that it would be tackle football over the rock-laden beaches of Western Alaska, I was sure nothing would come of it other than a chopper ride to the mainland and a medevac to Anchorage. But I was anxious for some elbowroom off the boat and so agreed to the game. Never having been the most fleet of foot, I completely expected to be crushed like a tomato by these behemoths. But no, usually a bit gawky and uncoordinated, my saving grace this time was my amazing speed and agility, especially after a few downs, when these mountains of men were left in their tracks gulping for oxygen. I slashed and dodged and cut my way through them like Walter Payton. It was the only time in my life I was *that* guy—the speedster, barely touched and with nary a scratch, returning to the boat both victorious and unscathed.

12

FALSE START

LANCER, JUNE 1984

I **DID NOT FARE** quite so well that early morning back in Seward, setting out on my first voyage.

When we arrived at the dock, Woody was on deck talking with one of the other skippers, not much older than myself and still dressed in his street clothes. At their feet played a young beagle, which Woody would occasionally kick away when it became too rambunctious.

Mark and I stood on the dock with our bags until their conversation was finished. I gathered that the skippers were discussing the storm clouds building to the west, and it seemed that the younger skipper was opting to stay put until the skies looked better before heading out.

I felt an immediate sense of relief. Maybe we'd wait too and I'd have the reprieve I suddenly found myself looking for.

"I haven't missed an opening in forty years," growled Woody, "and I'm not about to start now."

"All right, we'll see you out there," said the other skipper, nodding as he passed and headed for home. It was only then that Woody finally turned and asked how we were doing.

"Okay," said Mark. "Weather looking bad?"

"Not yet," said Woody, his voice, as always, containing that edge, that something sharp and gravelly that immediately put me on the defensive. Mark asked about the little dog and was informed he would indeed be coming along and that he went by the moniker of Pinocchio Stinky Sanchez, or *Mr.* Sanchez, to us.

"What are you standing there for?" Woody finally barked. "Better come aboard and stow your gear. And don't worry," he added, "we'll be across the gulf and anchored before the weather hits. Who knows? We might even be the only ones on the fishing grounds."

As we climbed aboard and made our way through the galley, turning sideways to slide our bags by the tiny table, it was difficult to erase the persistent dread I had woken up feeling. It had not dissipated but had grown as we'd neared the docks and as the time finally came to head out. I looked around the cabin—a much tighter fit than I'd remembered. To a landlubber like me it resembled the smallest of travel trailers. The big tenders would be luxurious compared to this, the *Lancer*'s little seating area, a sink and stove shoehorned onto the opposite wall, and all of it surrounded by a variety of makeshift cupboards and shelves stuffed with books, papers, and canned goods. On a small vessel like this the wheel and a cadre of electronics—radios, radar, and LORAN—shared what little space there was with the galley, encircling the boat's large front windows. And directly below was the ladder that led to our sleeping quarters. At first glance, it was a dark claustrophobic cell: four tight bunks contoured to the prow of the boat, each with a miniature mesh hammock swinging above just big enough for immediate possessions—perhaps a book, glasses, and hat. As I would find out soon enough, it was a chamber subject to all sorts of strange boat noises—water lapping against the hull, lines moaning in the wind, the echo of the anchor chain lurching against its roller.

Mark threw his gear on one of the bunks and I threw mine atop another.

"Goddamnit!" Caught completely unaware, I staggered and turned to see Woody's face, beet red, bearing down on me from the hole above the ladder. "That's my bunk," he bellowed.

"Sorry," I stammered, but he was gone before I could utter another word. There was still time to make a break for it—to turn and just take off running down the dock and never look back—but time was quickly drawing to a close and soon it would be entirely too late.

When I finally mustered enough courage to climb back on deck he asked us if we had everything—especially our crew licenses. But being so new to the state and to commercial fishing, neither of us even knew they were required.

Woody just stood there for a moment glaring at us and shaking his head in disbelief. At last he pulled a wad of grease-stained bills from his pants and unrolled one for each of us. A hundred, he said. A draw against our wages. He'd already explained that we'd each get fifteen percent of the catch—after the cost of food and fuel. I didn't know exactly what that meant but Mark assured me it was good.

While Woody and The Quiet Man went to buy groceries, Mark and I headed to a nearby fishing supply shop. After my license, there was enough left over to purchase a cheap pair of rubber boots, which Mark informed me I would need. No one, of course, bothered to tell me about raingear. Like boots, it's assumed that a fisherman has his own. Luckily, some hapless crewman had left his behind on the *Lancer*, though that I needed to use them would prove to be a continual point of censure.

Once we were back on board, I watched as Mark and The Quiet Man untied the boat and stowed the lines. This done, I followed them into the cabin as Woody maneuvered out of the harbor. There was no looking back now.

13

THE OLD MAN AND THE SEA

WOODY SEEMED COMPLETELY uninterested in answering questions. Instead, he was intent on listening to one of the two radios blasting the scuttlebutt of fishermen and the mechanical drone of the marine weather channel. I had no way of knowing that it would take two to three hours just to motor outside the bay and another three hours, under the best conditions, to cross the Gulf and reach the fishing grounds in Lower Cook Inlet. Already conditions had become choppy, the clouds angling closer. And Mark and The Quiet Man seemed to have disappeared. Apparently they had gone below, retreating into the darkness of their bunks and leaving me completely alone with Woody. At the time, the thought of being cooped up down there next to the roar of the engine room, breathing diesel fumes and subject to the full impact of each wave, seemed incomprehensible—especially when there was so much to see up here. I had yet to learn that the bunk is your one and only private space aboard a boat and that unless a job needs immediate attention, it's a brief sanctuary where you can usually remain undisturbed.

There was little else to do but fasten myself to a seat at the table. Mr. Sanchez huddled, shaking, against my leg, as ill at ease as I was in feeling the pitch and roll of the waves; these steadily increased as we neared the Gulf. By the time we reached the head of the bay, the sky had grown completely dark and the sea angry. The small boat pounded into each swell, the seas building until finally a bitter spray was thrown over the bow and slammed onto the outside of the cabin windows, it's splash temporarily blinding us and sending Woody off on a long tangent of expletives.

The further we traveled, the more cantankerous and infuriated the forces of nature—and Woody—seemed to become. With every flex of the ocean's muscle we would again barrel down another watery slope, and all I could do was watch as Woody, like a madman at the helm, tried to hold us on course, stamping his feet and cursing the weather, and kicking Mr. Sanchez back under the table when the poor dog came out to seek comfort under his legs. I couldn't help but wonder if it was like this all the time. Was Woody like this all the time, screaming and pounding his fists? Was this what we were expected to fish in? Could you even set gear in this?

In truth, Woody's demeanor should have been a clue that this was anything but normal. With each violent thrust of wind and the increasing pitch of each wave, the more infuriated he became. But his fury finally reached its pinnacle as we sailed down the backside of another steep wall of water. This time the propeller protested in a sharp whine as it went momentarily dry, the whole boat feeling as though it was about to be spun in a new direction. Then objects that looked as though they had been on the shelves for more than a decade began to crash to the floor.

Somehow I managed to pry my fingers loose from the edge of the table and stagger to my feet, trying in vain to maintain my balance and restore what I could to the shelves. I'd return something to its rightful place, only for it to tumble free again. Each time it came crashing to the floor, it would set Woody off on another tirade, cursing and stamping, and this time his anger directed solely toward me. I'd never had anyone speak to me like this. "Goddamnit," he yelled. "Pick this stuff up. No, this stuff. What are you, an idiot? The stuff that's going to spill! Goddamnit. In the sink. Leave the rest. Goddamn you."

I could feel the fear rising—the sweat beginning to trickle down my sides. And it wasn't necessarily fear of the sea. I have no doubt Woody had had his share of Oh Shit Moments and this might even have been one of them. But I had nothing to compare it to—no frame of reference. I was too ignorant to know if I even ought to be scared. No, this was the beginning of a course that had been set down for our entire voyage, where I was oblivious to any real danger and instead suspicious of this crazy old man. He seemed insane to me, making me leery of this entire untenable circumstance I found myself in. . . . How had I ended up here? How had I allowed this to happen? And where the hell were the other guys? How could they still be in their bunks?

I may even have begun to pray, making all those promises that would never be kept—to give up simple pleasures and to make amends to those I'd wronged. I would do anything so as to never intrude upon this world again. So that I might find myself elsewhere, anywhere, so long as it was comfortable and out of reach of this crazy old bastard.

It was truly a living hell—one that seemed to wear on into eternity. Yet like all things, after four or five interminable hours in the Gulf the welcome sight of land at last filtered into view. As we rounded a substantial outcropping and glided into sheltered water in one of the many coves that dot the vast and rocky shores of Lower Cook Inlet, The Quiet Man and Mark finally emerged from their lair. They looked rather haggard and somewhat surprised at the debris scattered around the cabin. As they headed out to drop the anchor, I felt the tension loosen slightly with the company and likely Woody's own sense of relief at having made it to calm water. The boat was at last secured amidst a fortress of steep brush-covered cliffs, each with its own waterfall cascading gracefully into the calm green pools of the cove. How could a storm rage outside a place so peaceful, its surface disturbed by what was now only a low-lying fog rising like dust in the dim footlights of some mystic stage? There was no one in sight and the radios were silent. Only the soft hum of the generator could be heard, along with the occasional bickering of gulls overhead, replacing the all-consuming din of the diesel engine down below.

As the boat swung on its anchor I lost a sense of which direction we had come from and where Seward lay. Under other circumstances I would have been mesmerized by the sublime beauty in front of me, but the crossing had left me shaken and filled with desolation and foreboding, and I realized an underlying but stifling tension still eclipsed the entire cabin.

The others sensed it too, the way they looked back and forth from Woody to me. Only Mark spoke occasionally, trying without success to make small talk as we shared a dinner of soup and sandwiches. Woody hadn't said a word to me and I didn't dare speak to him. How could I even begin to explain what I'd witnessed while the others had slept—a situation far worse than fifty-knot winds and twenty-foot seas and more than likely just a taste of what was to come over the next several weeks?

• • •

The following morning I waited until the other two emerged from their bunks before making an appearance. The old man had prepared bacon, eggs, and pancakes—a pre-season tradition, he said, before getting down to business. He appeared to be in better spirits, his disposition settling into mere gruffness.

After breakfast, under a clearing sky, with its receding clouds and occasional wisps of warm sunlight, we began our day's work. After removing the skiff from the deck, the seine was threaded through the block and snaked out of the fish hold, falling in veils behind us, and stacked carefully onto the back deck. I wondered how on earth this enormous net would ever be laid out in anything but a tangled mess. For each new task I would seek some explanation, at first from The Quiet Man, who would casually brush me aside without guidance of any kind. "Just watch," he'd say, "you'll see." Mark didn't really know anything, although he did his best to fake it. And Woody, though he would try to describe certain facets of each job, would meet any attempt at clarification with growing impatience—once again baring his fangs. It was a far cry from the college classrooms I had until now studied in. Suddenly I found myself enrolled in the school of trial and error—an institution closely associated with that of hard knocks.

Still, most of that first day I would listen and try to pick up what I could. I did the dishes because I knew how to do them. I also practiced my knots. But with my growing consternation and fear of the old man it was impossible to even begin to let my guard down, much less take in what I was seeing and experience the wonder that such a place should inspire, surrounded as it was by some of the most truly spectacular scenery on the planet.

"Imagine," said Woody, as we cruised looking for jumpers. "All of this a park, a national park."

"Oh, that's good," I said, thinking I was agreeing with him.

"Good?" he said incredulously. "All this land tied up so no one can use it? What's good about that?"

I shrugged. *We're using it*, I thought—a remark wisely kept to myself.

"Day was," he went on, "when a man could come out here and build a cabin, mine for gold, go trapping. Can't anymore. Not with some damn college bureaucrat tellin' you what to do."

I just shrugged again, something I'd do a lot of on board the *Lancer*. As usual, I had said the wrong thing and it was too late to redeem myself. And I couldn't tell him what I really thought. Truth was, it was like no place I had ever seen—untouched and not the least sign of humanity anywhere.

Woody assured us that would change soon enough. By nightfall there would be at least a dozen other boats tooling around now that the storm had broken and fishing was about to begin.

We continued to scout for jumpers—salmon that mysteriously launched themselves up, sometimes three or four feet above the surface—which were usually indicative of a school. Although Woody had all the latest electronic gadgets designed for spotting salmon, he told us he relied mostly on feel, an interior sonar honed over a lifetime of hunting for fish. But we had yet to see a single jumper and he wasn't feeling like there were many around.

"Just as well," said the old man, "it's early and we're going to need a lot of practice setting the gear." The thought of this once again overshadowed any sense of awe I should have felt cruising these glacier-carved fjords, eagles riding the thermals overhead, and porpoises riding our wake below. My spirit felt further smothered each time I was castigated for not knowing how to do the simplest chore, an invisible hand looping my intestines into knots—bowline, fisherman's bend, clove hitch—making these the most trying days of my short life. And really, what hope was there for tomorrow, when the real work was scheduled to begin and money was on the line?

14

ALL THE *WRONG* MOVES

IT WAS A rude awakening, rousted at six by the loud choking of the
diesel. Seeing Mark and The Quiet Man jump out of their bunks
and hurry into their clothes, I followed suit, grabbing coffee and
heading out onto deck to set up for the day. Mark arranged the
skiff as best he could based on the limited information he had been
given. Skiff man was a key position, like a quarterback, who, once
he proves himself and gains a reputation, can demand more money
for his services. But Mark was a rookie and therefore apt to catch
a lot of flak from the coach when things went bad. Seining, when
done right, is a synchronized, well-crafted marine ballet. But like
any dance, it takes knowledge and experience, something that was
in very short supply on the *Lancer*. What wasn't in short supply was
tension. I could feel it build as we scouted, reaching its peak each
time Mark was instructed to climb over the seine and into the skiff.
I would ready myself on deck with a "quick release"—a cord that
I was to pull like a parachutist's rip-cord, cutting Mark loose and
sending him and our enormous net out into the ocean. The first of
many problems we would encounter was that the old man was up
on the fly bridge, facing forward; with the wind blowing and motor
blaring, he was completely impossible to hear and his sign lan-
guage a complete mystery. Was he waving at Mark to start the outboard, The Quiet Man to secure a line, or me to let it go? I learned
right away that the worst thing I could possibly do was release the

gear—and Mark—before it was time. Not only would that bring the wrath of Woody down upon me, but it would raise the ire of my fellow deckhands who were forced into at least an hour of hard labor for no reward—only a sore back. So I would wait until the point when Woody was completely irate, anger burning in his eyes, blood vessels about ready to burst, his mouth forming that word—goddamnit—only then, when I was completely sure, would I let her rip. I'd pull that cord and send Mark off, usually still trying to start his stubborn outboard. He'd be out there helpless, floundering, subject to the whim of the sea, The Quiet Man shaking his head in dismay and Woody on the fly bridge screaming his lungs out at his two greenhorn deckhands.

And if we were lucky enough to get the motor fired up and Mark actually circled in the right direction and we managed to somehow, miraculously, close a set up and make the ends of the net meet, that's when the real problems would begin. All of it was accompanied by a flurry of orders bellowed across the deck, terms I'd never heard before—the pucker line, the davit—describing things I'd never seen and until now didn't even know existed. With my slow response and Mark's, the seine would invariably slide under the boat or get hung up on some rocks, causing long delays and a lot of wasted effort.

At last, about midnight, after waiting for the rising tide to free our seine for the final time, we were allowed to retreat into the relative comfort of our bunks. With every muscle contracted and tightening, my young back throbbing, and the mystery of jellyfish stings tingling around my wrists and all over my face, I lay silently in that dark chamber listening to all the strange noises of the boat. Not only was I broken in a physical sense, but completely mentally and spiritually spent. I had never heard the term *screamer* before. But I now knew the meaning of it, and why Woody had needed two deckhands just days before the season opened.

15

MAKING ENDS MEET

ILIAMNA BAY, APRIL 1997

WE WERE ANCHORED behind Augustine Island before nightfall. It was remarkably calm—so calm, Tim decided not to post anyone on anchor watch. We had electronics that could draw an invisible circle around the boat and an alarm would sound if we breached its perimeter, but it had no way of letting us know if another vessel was dragging down upon us. I'd been here before with hundreds of boats lined up in the small gut behind the island—the darkness illuminated by the eerie glow of their giant halogen lights, the industrial hum of generators rising in unison, transforming this no man's land into a precarious floating metropolis—and I knew catastrophe was always right around the corner. Radios would blare, warning adrift boats that they were quickly heading toward someone else; time and again, in the middle of the night I would be stirred out of bed from a restless sleep to pull or reset the anchor. It was often hardly worth the bother of getting undressed between episodes.

Yet it seemed that at least for the time being we'd be safe. And with the motor silenced on the *Iliamna Bay*, talk flowed easily. I found Brad shared my love of fly fishing. In fact, that's what brought him to Alaska; he'd been visiting friends for a few weeks when he stumbled upon Tim, who had recently let a deckhand go. Eight hours later, he was heading out to spend the summer seining. Of course, we discussed commercial fishing, family, and even politics, with the liveliest debate revolving around coffee. Tim insisted on canned, Karl the fresh stuff, and Brad and I sided with Karl.

The next day we would be test fishing; the Department of Fish and Game in their constant vigil to see if the herring were ripe and to determine when they should call an opening, asked for volunteers. Tim signed us up mainly so he might check our skills and see how we worked together. With just a bit of explanation and patience, and like the experienced crew we were, it was magic. The seine closed up and pursed as if we'd been working together for years. Without the pressure of a big payoff, it was leisurely fishing, spread among several boats over the next couple of days. Once Tim was satisfied we were ready for the task, and with the Department of Fish and Game's test fishing and sampling showing that the herring roe was far from ripe—meaning we would remain on twenty-four-hour notice—he decided to take the *Iliamna Bay* into the mouth of the nearby Paint River.

"I love this boat," Karl remarked as we motored into the Paint, "the way it's low-slung, and how that makes it ride." This, along with the boat's relatively flat bottom, would allow us the luxury of going periodically dry in the river mouth, immune from the fiasco that commenced with the changing weather around Augustine.

Our first night in the river we heard it: pleading on the radio, many times over, for someone to fire up a dragging boat before it crashed into another. What a relief not to have to deal with it, to have easy access to shore and long walks, biding our time in the hurry-up-and-wait game of herring seining. Now I was glad Karl and Brad had brought some extra whiskey. There were no worries breaking Tim's one-drink rule here when walking the shore. One evening we even hiked to the nearby McNeil River Sanctuary, where the wildlife viewers and photographers lucky enough to be chosen by a lottery—so as not to encroach on the wildlife—came to watch brown bears. Often twenty to thirty grizzlies at a time would gather to feast on the annual glut of returning salmon. But that would be mid-summer, a long way off. For us there was still a crusty blanket of snow, the park buildings boarded up as we roamed the treeless, windswept grounds of the wilderness camp in full raingear, happily swapping stories. I shared my ignoble introduction to fishing, and Karl told us of his start—one much more inviting and profitable than mine.

He told us of his fateful lift with that old family friend, the one he had described to me on the dock back in Homer, who had known his brother and had delivered him to the Osmar family's quintessential Alaskan homestead, with its longstanding and successful setnet operation. He'd picked fish there each summer for the next eight years, paying his way through college and later financing the start of a family, earning enough to eventually buy his own setnet sites in the mid 1980s.

"It was unbelievable," he reminisced as we walked the beach. I listened, curious how he'd made out during what was likely the heyday of Cook Inlet fishing. Crown Royal—Clown Oil, he called it—burned at the back of my throat, the cold slap of wind on my cheeks.

"It was a lot like now," he said, referring to the wind. "My face hurt, only from smiling so much. Three dollars a pound, that's what we were being paid for salmon."

"Nice," I said. I'd gotten paid that myself, but never when there was a lot of fish and big hauls being taken in.

"Yeah, those first three years we thought we'd hit the mother lode. We were filling three skiffs with $20,000 worth of fish, *at each tide*. For a while we were making $120,000 an opening."

Hearing this I couldn't help but wonder how it was I always seemed to miss these really big payoffs. Maybe I hadn't looked hard enough. Or was I just too easily satisfied? Like the fish hippies back in the cannery, if I'd earned enough to travel or to hole up somewhere and read the *Iliad* or make an attempt at *Finnegan's Wake*, that was enough for me. It was easy to convince myself I wasn't being lazy—that this haphazard pursuit of knowledge was noble. This was a sure sign that somewhere along the way I had contracted "Seasonal Work Syndrome."

Once I tried to explain this to them. Brad understood, but Karl and Tim just kind of looked at me askance. They both had time off and plenty of money to enjoy it, but I could see that neither of them would ever even entertain the thought of such a thing. No one could ever accuse either of them of being lazy, but like many fishermen they probably had to justify to others such large spans of time—usually during the winter—when they weren't actually bringing in any money. "I'm busy," Karl said, somewhat defensively when I brought this up. "We spent a lot of effort building a house, and sure, we've been luckier than most in that we've had a lot of time to spend with the kids, but that's a big job."

And Tim agreed. You could tell he was the type that needed to keep busy by rebuilding an engine or working on the boat. "There's always something that needs to be done," he said.

After nearly two weeks of waiting, hiking in the rain, eating, even when we weren't hungry, playing endless word games and solving crossword puzzles, it finally looked like we would have an opening. At six-hour notice we emerged from our safe haven, and at one-hour a squadron of spotter planes took flight, radioing down information on where the dark clouds of fish were and where we might set. We'd stepped up, all at once, from complacently biding our time to full-bore adrenaline-stoked mania. And it didn't matter how many times you'd been through this, the most experienced, saltiest of old salts' blood would percolate with the countdown over the radio, 5-4-3-2-1, and then only twenty minutes to set—one opportunity and one opportunity only to get it right. One single, slim chance at payday.

"Now, Tim, now," I heard the pilot screaming from above.

"Got 'em," said Tim as we began laying the nets out, nearly colliding with another boat setting on the same fish. Our co-op partners were nowhere in sight, making sets of their own. If they hadn't been, if it had been deemed there were not enough herring to go around, they would be over here with us, risking their boats, trying to ward off the other vessels.

But they weren't, so we laid out next to our competitor; Karl and the other skiffman dueled like dragsters before circling in opposite directions. We hoped Karl corralled most of the herring onto our side of the nets. In no time, we closed and adroitly sealed off our ring of gear and stacked corks and leadline on deck, watching our circle of net shrink and hoping that as it grew smaller we would see breaking the surface the thousands of tiny dimples that signi-fied we had some fish. That's when the action really began. Low-ered to the water in a small rubber Zodiak with a fifteen-horse out-board and piled high with buoy balls, each with its own carabiner, I motored around the net, subjected to the wakes of nearby seine boats and tenders. I would look up at their giant hulls towering above my little craft like hungry sea monsters as I buzzed around, attaching buoys anywhere the line was being pulled down and where I thought fish might escape. It was crazy, thrilling, and fun—and lucrative, we hoped, for there was always the chance that the fish weren't ripe and we'd have to release them.

Apparently we'd set well. The boat beside us came up nearly empty, while we looked like we had a substantial catch. After several roe technicians from the cannery sampled our fish and were satis-fied at its maturity, we were allowed to pump into the tenders that had attached themselves to the other side of our net. A hundred and twenty tons. Not bad. And with our co-op partners pulling in forty and twenty-five tons respectively, and at the expected price of around three hundred dollars a ton, I alone had likely made several thousand dollars. Not a bad start.

16

BETTER THAN PRISON

LANCER, JUNE 1984

THE DAYS STRETCHED unbearably long. The time between openings was spent mending gear, scraping paint, and cleaning the engine room of the *Lancer*. The nights were cut unmercifully short by the confounded sound of the diesel sputtering to life—Lucifer's own alarm clock signaling yet another day in Hell. Mark insisted in his quiet, hardened way that things weren't really that bad, that prison—as if we'd all been there a couple of times—was much worse. I wasn't so sure. My cell mates here were an odd bunch to be sure. Woody, for instance, hadn't crawled into his bunk the entire time we'd been on this trip. He'd merely close his eyes periodically, nodding at the galley table. Perhaps it was the Titanic-sized cups of coffee he drank all day, prepared camp-style with the cheapest grounds boiled to bitter perfection. He accused me of not being much of a coffee drinker—a lightweight, he called me, as I consumed only about a gallon of the stuff a day and was forced to mix it with large amounts of milk in order to tame it somewhat.

At least we were beginning to catch a few fish. And it never ceased to amaze me that this incredible pile of net would actually unfurl the way it was supposed to—stretching into a wall and actually enclosing salmon. Of course, our sets were still far from smooth and graceful but we were improving. How could we not when we were attempting as many as twenty sets during a twenty-four-hour opening? It was an unheard of number that would send The Quiet Man cringing and swearing, especially whenever we came up empty, which we did more often than not. He was the only member of the three-man crew who realized how excessive our labors actually were. I would spend most waking hours looking at the snow-capped peaks, not to take in their beauty but to plot my escape. I actually thought that if I made it over a certain mountain pass and walked the right beaches at low tide, I would somehow make it back to Seward. I would only have to fend for myself for a week or two through some of the densest wilderness in North America.

Occasionally Mark and I would take a break, driving the skiff to shore on the pretense of taking Mr. Sanchez for a walk. These were the least trying of trying times, a pause between jobs, between torment and despair. I could see daydreams were Mark's way of coping, still talking about the cabin he would build and the start of a new life. He did his best to keep me going through all this, sidling up to me on deck and whispering conspiratorially, "Hey, why don't we see what happens if we let the skiff go?" or "Next time the old man's asleep at the table why don't you tie his shoelaces to his chair, then I'll holler for him to come out here." Stupid little things, but it brought us together—us against them and uniting Mark and me.

On the whole, the voyage had not gotten much better, but I had at least begun to settle in, thinking I'd seen and endured the worst. That was when Mark casually glanced out the window and commented that the shoreline looked a little close. All at once, in a firestorm of cursing, Woody went for the helm, nearly throwing Mark to the floor in the process. I had no idea how close to disaster we were until Mark and I scurried onto the bow. The boulder-ridden shore was nearly within arm's reach. By then I'd helped drop and raise anchor enough to realize what was wrong: there was a complete lack of pressure, no hydraulic whine—the anchor was gone, it's old rusty cable, after years of use and neglect, had given out. As I started to guide the inch-thick cable onto its roller, I remembered a recurring dream that I'd been having since the first time I'd dropped the anchor. In the dream we'd release the break, and as we did in real life, sometimes we'd pound on the anchor with a heavy ball-peen hammer to release it from its chock. In the dream though, somehow I became impaled or attached to one of its flukes and was pulled downward, enveloped by the dark sea. My only hope of release was in waking up.

Once we had the limp anchor line winched in, Mark and I stood and watched Woody through the front windows. We heard him coax the cold diesel to life, solid and uncustomarily calm as he slid her into gear and maneuvered the boat between a maze of towering rocks—barely averting disaster. Fortunately, we hadn't been sleeping when we lost the anchor. Unfortunately, with only a small yachtsman's anchor as backup, after long days of work we would have to remain awake in pairs, running the boat throughout the night. For a short time I thought this might be the stroke of luck I was looking for—my ticket back to Seward and a golden opportunity to get off the *Lancer*. But with an emergency opening being called in another area and the prospect of catching fish outweighing the cost of burning fuel, any hopes of escape were dashed.

Since Mark and I had the least experience, it was only logical that we be split up on these nights. I, of course, would be teamed with Woody and Mr. Sanchez, whose disposition had grown as irascible as his owner's. I couldn't think of anything worse than being alone with them, especially after losing an anchor. Yet it was probably for the best. The Quiet Man would have likely just let me run the boat aground. At least Woody would, in no uncertain terms, let me know what was coming.

So, with a brief lesson on reading the radar and following a computerized track of dots and lines on the plotter, I was told to take the helm and did my best to keep my nerves in check while maintaining course. With only a narrow corridor of black sea glistening in the floodlights, I would trust that the magic display of electronics was right. Night after night, Woody dozed at the table, waking periodically with a start. "Goddamnit! Where the hell are we? You keeping an eye on things?" Every night it was the same. At least once he would ask where I was from. "New York? Jesus Christ, what in the hell are you doing here?"

One evening, not wanting to disturb Woody asleep at the table or the others down below, I stayed on watch. In the morning, Woody asked me what the hell I was doing. "Well, you better be able to work today," he said, but I detected just a trace of respect in his voice. On board the *Lancer* that would have to do.

After several nights of wheel watch in pairs, there was a short break scheduled between openings and the crew thought we might at last be headed home. Yet much to everyone's chagrin, instead of heading to town and buying a new anchor, Woody decided to cruise for two hours, returning to the cove where he had first noticed us drifting. With only the slimmest of hopes, he decided to begin a search for our wayward anchor. Needless to say, there was a good deal of bellyaching—even within earshot of Woody—as we scratched the bottom of the ocean floor with a grapnel anchor borrowed from another boat. "We're wasting our time," grumbled The Quiet Man, but after only a handful of passes we hooked onto something. We each took a wager on what it was: an abandoned crab pot, a piece of a lost ship, buried treasure. When we saw our needle of an anchor returned from its twelve fathom haystack, even Woody was astounded.

• • •

The lack of sleep and long days of work finally began to pull at me. On deck I continued to stack corks or coil line, my eyes closing periodically; I lingered someplace between lightness and darkness. That evening, for the first time in the two weeks since we'd been out, I left the dinner dishes. It was seven o'clock and to hell with them, I was going below and hitting the rack.

When I finally awoke the diesel engine was pounding in my brain. I had actually slept through that abominable starting of the engine. There was another body, The Quiet Man, huddled in the bunk across from me. Through the hatch above, sunshine poured in around Woody's legs. He was at the helm and I'd have to ask him to let me by. I hated to ask even the simplest thing of him, like stepping aside so I might stumble out on deck to take a leak. But there was no other option.

"Goddamnit!" he bellowed when I tapped his leg. "Thought maybe you were dead down there. Goddamn sleeping beauty."

Bleary-eyed and hazy, I crawled out and looked at the clock. It was almost noon—out cold for nearly fifteen hours. "Where are we?" I asked.

"Where in the hell do you think we are? Goddamnit, we're on our way to town."

I looked outside, and sure enough, we were in the Gulf—only this time it was calm, with seabirds casually swaying overhead and two or three other seiners to our portside. They were heading home as well. Finally. I couldn't believe it, my ordeal was about to come to an end.

I took my coffee outside and joined Mark on the fly bridge, where he was the epitome of comfort: leaning back on a cushion, feet up on the rail, and one of the special cigars he'd been saving dangling from his mouth. "How are you doing?" he asked, handing me one as I sat down to join him. I did my best to assume a like demeanor, taking in the distant mountains, watching as those to starboard slowly slipped from view and those bordering the mouth of Resurrection Bay slowly began to take their place. An appropriate name I thought, Resurrection Bay. Probably given by some beaten down mariner like myself, reborn at the sight of these waters.

Sitting back, I let the sun envelop me, silently basking in its warm glory as I partook of the delightful and unexpected joy of a cigar, savoring its sweet smoky aroma, which mixed with the bitter flavor of Woody's coffee. It was an intoxicating combination. It made the world seem reasonable—for the first time, almost pleasant. But no, I couldn't allow myself to be duped. Not by something as simple as a cup of coffee, a smoke, some sleep, and the prospect of a few days off. No, as soon as I set foot on land, that's where I would remain. As quick as I could blink an eye, I'd be off this tub.

• • •

With several thousand pounds of fish to unload, we motored in to the large dock in front of the cannery. Stationed on the bow, line in hand, I stood ready to fasten the *Lancer* to the pier with one of my repertoire of knots. I still had to nervously think about each one, but I could at least tie them. The Quiet Man was at the stern, bored and indifferent, waiting to tie his end. Woody had taken his place, towering above me at the fly wheel, guiding the boat into a tight spot between two tenders.

Once we tied off, we were immediately greeted by a dock crew from the cannery. I was pleasantly surprised to find that this was not at all like unloading at sea onto a tender, where we had to pitch all the fish and clean the hold ourselves. Here, the six-dollar-an-hour cannery workers did all the work for us while Mark and I stood around on deck and fielded questions from them, feeling for the first time like real fishermen. We asked after our friends and Mark's wife. Yeah, they knew them, but they were likely inside toiling away, and would be there until ten or eleven that night. It was pretty heady, standing on deck as a fisherman—at least for now. But all the while I was trying to think of when might be the right time to tell Woody I was through.

It was a pretty quick process, and before I knew it we were unloaded and back at the harbor proper, the *Lancer* secure in its slip. *Now*, I thought, *now's the time*.

"You guys can stay on the boat," offered Woody, his voice more amiable than I'd heard since we'd left.

"I've got to find Faye," said Mark, "and see when she gets off work."

"And I'm headed to the campground," I added. The last place on Earth I wanted to stay was the *Lancer*. The time had come, best get it over with.

"All righty then," said the old man, "I'll lock her up. How are you guys set for money?"

Mark turned to look at me. "I think we could both use some," he said.

Woody marched us over to the cannery office, where he was heading anyway, to sign for some cash—a draw against the fish we had caught. I have no idea how much he received, but after emerging from an inner office, he counted out five bills each—first to Mark and then to me. Five one hundred dollar bills. It was more than I had seen in a long time, and Mark and I tried our best to stay poker-faced, sneaking just a sidelong glance at each other in acknowledgment of our unanticipated wealth.

Well, you can hardly tell someone you've quit, not when he's just doled out five hundred bucks. It would just have to wait.

"Have a good time," he said, seeing us off, "but not *too* good a time. And remember, I want to see you back on the boat at nine in the morning, day after tomorrow."

It's difficult to even begin to imagine how truly magnificent that first breath of freedom tasted—even the fishy taste of dockside air. And it was made all the more sweet watching those less fortunate, these poor dock workers chained to the unloading of boats until the wee hours of the morning. Those poor bastards would have to work while Mark and I, a thousand dollars richer, waltzed off in front of them ready to have a good time, at least for now the captains of our own fate.

17

IGNORING OMENS

ILIAMNA BAY, APRIL 1997

THE OTHER TWO boats in our co-op, the *Rafferty* and *Sea Mist*, were both faster and already had the jump on us as they headed west. And though we had a five or six day journey ahead of us, Tim was in a hurry to get going. He prodded Karl and me to work faster bundling up our seine onto a wooden pallet, to then be loaded onto a tender alongside us. Our other, slightly larger seine, the one we had bundled up back in Homer—one more suited to fishing the bigger herring in Bristol Bay—had been shipped by the cannery and was likely waiting for us in Togiak. Karl reminded Tim of the lengthy journey ahead and that we didn't want this 6,000-pound net to fall on anyone's head because we had been rushed.

"Sorry," said Tim, "I'm always like this before heading out west." But the opening in Cook Inlet had started later than usual and he knew that no one was going to wait for stragglers. After spending so much money on fuel and supplies the last thing he wanted was to miss an opening. Also, a big low-pressure system was moving in, looking like it might slow us down as well. Plus, this was the most risky part of our trip coming up—heading around the Aleutian Islands and then crossing the Bering Sea in a small boat.

Initially, between Kodiak Island and the mainland was Shelikof Strait, which with a storm brewing was a veritable funnel for bad weather and high seas. And it would be several days later before we reached the formidable Bering Sea, which due to its relative shallowness and position among far-northern mountain ranges and archipelagos is the very place where extreme weather originates. It is the birthplace of the Pacific storms that rock even the coasts of the Hawaiian Islands and Japan.

First on watch, I decided it was definitely a night to stand my two hours and wake my relief right away. On a dark, moonless night with winds to what seemed near hurricane force, the seas built to the point where there was no choice but to regularly throttle down, slowing the boat to keep pace with them. All the while I continued keeping track of a small dot on the radar—happy to have another boat to follow out west—and watching for another larger bleep, likely a trawler or tanker motoring our way, careful to stay out of its path.

When my two hours were up I immediately went to roust Tim, who was next on watch. I didn't like waking him up. Not because he was the skipper but because he was difficult to summon from a deep sleep—something I hadn't seen in too many captains. I'm sure if there had been panic in my voice he would have jumped from bed ready for action, but gently trying to wake him took some doing. He slept hard and obviously didn't like being woken up. Maybe it was his long days at sea, but even when we dropped anchor he didn't wait long to see if we were holding; as soon as he was confident we were staying put he hit the rack right away.

• • •

When I woke up the water was still pretty rough—too rough to cook breakfast, so cold cereal would have to do. Fortunately the clouds had parted, dawn was breaking, and the storm had subsided to the point where it was merely a nuisance. Still it was tough to stand. Brad was at the wheel and Karl at the table with a cup of coffee.

"Man, we got our ass kicked last night," Karl remarked. I assumed he was making conversation and I just tried to maintain my balance long enough to get a cup of coffee myself.

"Did you hear the commotion?"

"What, with this motor running?"

"How about fire? Did you smell anything burning?"

"No," I said. He had my attention now. "What the hell happened?"

"I thought the boat was on fire, that's what happened."

"What?" I asked. Karl's expression was much closer to bemusement than terror. I knew there was no way I'd sleep through such a potential catastrophe, but I was curious.

"Did you hear any of this?" I asked Brad.

"No," he said, looking around the cabin. "Obviously the boat wasn't on fire."

"Something was burning," said Karl.

"Mostly your imagination," said Brad. "Thankfully."

"Well, I did wake up from a dream, that's true," said Karl, "but it was this really vivid dream that the engine room was on fire, and when I woke up I really smelled something burning, like something electrical. There was smoke down below. I can't believe it didn't wake you guys up."

Brad and I simply looked at each other and shrugged. The thrum of the motor was still keeping talk to a minimum, so we let Karl continue.

"So, I'm in a panic," he went on, "crawling across the cabin floor, you know, trying to keep low, heading for the door, and I look up and see Tim standing there cracking up. He'd just pulled one of our rubber gloves off the stove. It fell off the clothesline in the storm. He was just standing there laughing."

"I probably would have been too," I said, beginning to laugh myself, picturing Karl, dim-eyed and sleep-deprived, crawling across the floor. But I could still appreciate his terror, though it was something I didn't want to acknowledge. For some guys—guys who had been out for too long and burned themselves out—something like that can seem like an omen. But to them anything can seem like an omen, like the derelict boat that ran aground off of False Pass on the Aleutians. A boat belongs on the sea, not crippled on shore, and passing it—seeing a once-proud vessel stripped bare—it gives you an eerie feeling. But you always see stuff like that, and things like the glove falling on the stove, that always happens on boats. You need to ignore it. It's not an omen.

18

JUST LIKE A REAL FISHERMAN

LANCER, JUNE 1984

A **SERIES OF BELLS,** ringers, buzzers, the echo of alarms tolled from all
points of the compass—the anguished moans of cannery workers
on the rise. They'd all be at work when Mark showed up a few hours
later. I hadn't seen him since the night before last, leaving the Yukon
Bar after having put a good dent in our draws.

We'd started right away, despite a sign in the cannery's
Fisherman's Lounge that forbid alcohol. Another sign proclaimed:
THIS FACILITY FOR THE EXCLUSIVE USE OF FISHERMEN ONLY. EMPLOYEES CAUGHT
IN LOUNGE WILL BE TERMINATED. Imagine that—the place we'd headed
for our much-needed showers was off limits to a certain segment
of society, off limits to my friends. This was also about the time one
of the old hands from the cannery came rushing up to us, one of
those early visitors around our campground fire who had doled out
advice as if he were doing us a favor. Now he addressed us with
respect, the envy in his voice unmistakable as he bombarded us
with questions about where we had been and how the fishing was
shaping up.

It continued at the bars, buying rounds for each other and
receiving many offered up by extremely lubricated deckhands and
captains, fishermen likely better-off financially than us. The bars
were packed with them.

"What boat you off of?"

"The *Lancer*," we'd reply, each time surprised by the pride and conviction in our voices.

"Ah, Woody," more often than not would be the reply.

"You know Woody?" Mark asked one of them, a large, jolly, tattooed gentleman off one of the local boats.

"Sure," he said, "everybody knows Woody. He's a legend around here." To which Mark smiled. He liked the idea of being on a boat with a legend.

"How's the crew?" asked the fisherman.

"Great," said Mark.

"That's good," said the man, "Woody needs a group that will stay with him. Good fisherman, but he has a little trouble keeping a crew. But hey, you guys know all about that."

"We sure do," I said, laughing along with the fisherman, but I noticed Mark didn't think it very funny.

"A new guy throws things off for a while," the fisherman went on. "Even someone that's been fishing as long as Woody loses something if he can't keep a crew."

"Well, we plan on sticking it out," said Mark. "I think a guy could do pretty good with Woody."

"That's true," conceded the fisherman, "if you can deal with a screamer. Me, I can't. Been there and don't want to do that again. I'm on a great boat now and I'm not going anywhere. A family operation, mellow skipper, and best of all we co-op with his sons. If one boat does well, we all do."

"How do you get on a boat like that?" I asked.

"It ain't easy. Crew's mostly family, sons, daughters, cousins. They only hire hands they know well. I was lucky to get on with them and now that I am I ain't ever leaving."

"Sounds like he has a good gig," I remarked after he left.

"Ah, he's full of shit," Mark replied.

"You heard what he said about Woody not being able to keep a crew."

"Woody's a tough old bastard," said Mark, "I'll give you that, but we just need to hang in there. It'll pay off, you'll see."

I told Mark over and over again that I was done, finished, but each time he ignored me. Through each trip to the bar, every round of pool or darts, he just kept talking as if it were a given, that we were going back out and that was all there was to it. We'll have to do this or that to the boat he'd say, or he'd ask if I was all right with my bunk, offering to switch if I wanted. After a while there was no point in protesting—it was easier to tag along for just one night and enjoy being part of the fraternity. And that's just what it was, a fraternity. From the outset it was obvious. It would have been apparent to anyone that there was a conspicuous lack of women in every place we went. And those few that were around—including a bartender who must have been hauling in far more cash than any fisherman—were extremely popular. I could see from the outset, there was nothing to do but join the testosterone-fueled ruckus and make the most of it, because there wasn't the slightest chance I'd be leaving the bar with anyone but Mark.

I'll tell Woody tomorrow, I said to myself. The next day I even swung by the boat, but had to admit I was relieved to find no one there. It was locked up tight, meaning I could continue my recovery—and not just from a night of carousing but from the whole ordeal. So I quietly kept to myself in the corner of a coffee shop, savoring my tenuous autonomy and regaining at least some shred of independence, of self. Yet despite coming ashore, the ocean's constant sway continued to plague me. It had begun right away, before I even took a drink, from somewhere deep inside, and hadn't worn off. Mark assured me it was normal, that anyone who had been on a boat as long as we had might keep their sea legs for quite some time.

Even now, a couple days later, it was there, the tent rolling in unison to an invisible sea as I lay on my sleeping bag. Maybe when Mark came to pick me up I'd tell him I quit and not even have to see the old man—but he would never let me do that. Or, as chickenshit as it seemed, maybe I'd just make myself scarce. I could leave a note for Mark. I didn't know it then, but even that is more than a lot of hands would have done. But it was too late. Mark was outside the tent.

"Hey, you in there! We need to get down to the boat."

I was quiet for a moment, holding my breath.

"There's been some changes," he said.

You don't know the half of it, I thought, wondering is this it—do I tell him now? Or do I even consider the other option: getting up, taking one long last pull of freedom, and going with him?

I had finally gotten to catch up with my friends the night before. Unlike me, they were quiet, exhausted, and sober after a sixteen-hour workday. There was no chance of getting on at the cannery they said, and even if I did it sounded horrific, spending all day indoors, in dim light and shrouded in raingear, guillotining the heads off the salmon that poured in an endless rain from an overhead bin. It lasted until eleven o'clock every night. Lining fish into the maw of machines, the only consolation a fifteen-minute break every few hours. My friends told me when they closed their eyes it was all they saw: the machinery, the people—their mad, tired faces poking out under the yellow hoods of their raincoats, water dripping off their noses. And, of course, there were the fish—four hundred thousand pounds a day—following them into their dreams. The dreams I knew well, except in mine the fish were still alive, hoisted from the net, pounding against each other in the hold, pitched onto tenders, their last bit of life pulsating, convulsing in my hand before I threw them. And that's when I wasn't dreaming about lines or being caught on an anchor and dragged into the sea.

"What changes?" I quietly demanded from Mark as I emerged from the tent.

"All kinds of things," he said. "We've got a new deckhand, for one." Apparently The Quiet Man had taken off. "Just like that," declared Mark. "Woody's sure he's not coming back."

Imagine that, I thought. "Where have you been?"

"Met some friends, went to their house last night. Another late one. I'm paying for it now."

"Faye go with you? She didn't have to work?"

"I told her to quit. She's not made for that kind of work. She's going to stay with these friends we met—from Michigan, like me. Met another guy there, and when we get back from this trip I'm going to buy a truck from him—a pick-up with a camper. We're going to live in it while we save some money."

"Wow. Sounds like you plan on catching a lot of fish."

"It's an old truck. We gave him some money down and we'll give him the rest later. We'll have plenty by the end of the season."

I nodded, procrastinating, even at this point not sure what I would do.

"Let's get going," said Mark.

I stood there a minute considering—not whether I'd go or not but considering this strange place, so unlike the town of my youth where family and neighbors had resided for generations. No, here people were coming and going so quickly you had to meet them in a hurry, become fast friends posthaste, and after a day invite them to share your house or seal a deal on a truck with only a handshake. Or, it dawned on me, after only a couple of months together—or two weeks on a boat—come to depend on one another.

I turned slowly toward the tent. After paying my friends back some money I owed them, there was very little left. But there was something more than simply being broke again, something basic and essential behind all those wild pipedreams of Mark's. Perhaps I was going because of them, because they tied us together, because I actually believed in their simplicity. Also because it was clear Mark needed me out there, that we were a team—and I felt as if together we could face even Woody.

• • •

Mark filled me in on the way. Apparently Ray, our new deckhand, was not just Woody's friend but his *best* friend. I never liked The Quiet Man—especially his indifference—but at least he was a known entity, and for some reason the unknown always seems like it could be worse.

I'd find out soon enough. As we approached the dock there he was sitting on deck. He was a big man with dark hair and sharp chiseled features, his brown weathered face lifted toward the sun. As unbelievable as it seemed, I had come back. The only explanation I had was that maybe I was suffering from Stockholm Syndrome. Maybe I was the prisoner beginning to relate to my captors. Why else would someone subject himself to this? At least I was prepared with some extra raingear and a flashlight, so I could still read when Woody complained about the light from the little lamp above my bunk being on.

I climbed aboard and shook hands with Ray. He was half native, of Aleut descent. He was also a product of that long line of Norwegian fisherman who had made their way to Alaska sometime after the Russians. He was much closer to Woody's age than Mark's or mine, but had probably cut quite a dashing figure in his day. He said he hadn't been out on the water in years, almost apologizing before we even set off. I'd later find out that Woody had practically dragged him out with us thinking it would do him good to get away from Tony's Bar, where he was a regular. This habit of being at Tony's, or the interruption of it, showed in the way his big hands shook and in the way he steadied himself on deck.

As we headed out, I felt my fears concerning Ray slowly abating. He was everything The Quiet Man wasn't: amiable, easy-going, and full of jokes and stories. Interesting stories about the old days, about longshoring, deckhanding, trapping, and carousing. His performance on deck, however, was a bit shaky—at least at first—causing me to pick up the slack and work that much harder. But I didn't mind. You can't yell at your best friend—at least not often—and so Woody had to tone it down with me as well, especially when it was obvious that along with my work I was doing half of Ray's.

That didn't mean the screaming stopped altogether. It was a case of conditioning, I explained to Mark. I think we're like Pavlov's dog, I told him. When we don't get yelled at—goddamnit!—we know we've done something right and repeat it. Either because Ray was there, or because I was actually beginning to learn the ropes, at least the yelling was less frequent and at a lower decibel. It still didn't stop me from contemplating which mountain pass to climb over in order to make my escape, or thinking about chartering an airplane, or demanding to be put on the next company boat headed back to Seward. But I knew that I would then be the lowest of low, and my escape would be recounted in endless sea stories around these galley tables. Leaving in the middle of the trip went against every custom or unwritten law of the sea. It just wasn't done, except on the rare occasion when it was the whole crew. It didn't help watching some of the other boats. I looked on with envy at those with young skippers, the crew made up of friends who would laugh together and joke throughout the day—actually having fun while they worked. Sometimes the *Lancer* would tie up alongside them, share a meal, maybe barbecue a salmon on deck. Some of them complained about making eight or ten sets a day, and wouldn't believe us when we said we were still making sixteen or eighteen.

Though Woody was slightly more subdued, there continued to be plenty of jabs. Like when he told me to quit wasting batteries and demanded I turn off the goddamned light. That's when I brazenly produced my flashlight, announcing that I could now read as late as I wanted.

"Then how the hell you going to work tomorrow, if you stay up all goddamn night reading?" he said. But he left it at that.

And Mark was certainly not exempt, though he was usually out in the skiff for the worst of it, and unable to hear Woody calling him a dumbshit or idiot. "Not on your life," said Mark, when Woody suggested a radio. "It's bad enough seeing you, I really don't think I want to hear what you're saying."

Woody just looked at him askance, before letting out a big belly laugh. "No," he said, "you probably don't."

19

A GOOD OMEN AND
AN EARLY LESSON

ILIAMNA BAY, APRIL 1997

IT APPEARED THAT if Karl's bad dream and the burning glove were omens at all, they were good ones and had released any bad juju, as the weather continued to clear and the seas remained calm. And the good weather and good spirits held, even as we made our way through False Pass and looked upon that rusting hulk of an old boat, and even into the usually cantankerous Bering Sea. Our only concern now was our late start. Indeed it looked like an opening might be imminent. This caused Tim to run the engines much harder than he would have liked, gaining a few knots in the hopes we would reach the fishing grounds on time.

On our third or fourth full day of travel, my watch ended in the early morning just before sunrise and I roused Tim from his bunk. I had no problem staying awake on watch when it was really rough, but on calm nights it was difficult and this time required large amounts of caffeine. I was feeling its effects and realized there was no way I was going to fall asleep right away, so I decided to stay up with Tim for awhile. To make conversation I asked after the name of the *Iliamna Bay*.

"Well," Tim said. "It's kind of named in honor of my brother." He said it rather matter-of-factly, but Karl had mentioned, without going into detail, that Tim had lost a brother in a fishing accident in Cook Inlet. I thought I might have heard Tim mention him before.

"Is that the brother you came here with?" I asked.

"Yeah, my uncle Pat lived up here. I was just thirteen, my brother was nineteen—in college at the time—and we came up to fish on Uncle Pat's boat." Tim paused and looked distant, as if he were trying to recall the details.

"Is this something you'd rather not talk about?"

"No," said Tim. "It was a long time ago."

He was quiet a little while and I thought maybe that due to the engine noise he was giving up, the conversation dying and unraveling into thought as so many did. But then he began again. "Fishing had been slow and it was getting late in the season and Harvey—that was my brother—got an opportunity to tender. They'd wanted Uncle Pat, but he couldn't do it for some reason, so Harvey went. They had a radio, but this was back before people carried EPIRBs and survival suits."

He stopped again and asked me to fill his coffee. I thought he was done, but when I returned he began again.

"So no one really knows what happened. No one heard any radio calls and when they were overdue, the air services and a few boats began looking. Four or five days into it they found a couple of gas cans and later a few small pieces of the boat. Some of them washed up on Augustine Island."

"That's tough." What can you say to something like that? That wasn't far from where we'd been fishing either.

"As I said, it was a long time ago." But even over the din of the engine, I could tell from the tone in Tim's voice that it was fresh in his mind again.

"How'd you deal with it?"

"You'd think it would have affected me more, but I didn't really accept it for a few years. That's probably why I didn't push coming back to Alaska. As you can imagine, my parents had no intention of letting me come back. But later that's what I wanted. For whatever reason, this is what I want to do. The challenge, the outdoors. You know how it is—it's addictive. Working indoors is tough, it's like being tied down. Also," he added, "his death isn't something I still think about that much."

I nodded. It had been thirty years.

"Sometimes, though, on a long run," he continued, "when it's really rough, I'll think of him, even to the point of saying 'Hey, is this my turn now?' It did serve as an early lesson though. I've never had that attitude, that cowboy sort of thing. There's always been a certain exhilaration getting through a major storm but it's not like I conquered it. You can't conquer nature."

"That's for sure," I said. "It makes you begin to realize your limitations a little."

"It's also probably made me realize mine," said Tim. "I might go crabbing, for instance, but not on anything less than 150 feet. There's a lot of eighty- or one hundred-foot boats out there but I won't be on them. And you see recklessness all the time. You can't have reckless guys on a boat or somebody's going to get hurt." He paused again for a second. "Believe it or not, it's also strengthened my belief in God. You have to make good sound judgments, but ultimately He's in control. If I thought I was the only one in control, I wouldn't be here anymore."

20

LIKE THE PROS WE ARE

LANCER, JUNE 1984

O**N THE** *Lancer* there were no thoughts of a supreme being, only Woody. He was in charge. It's a good thing Mark was there, though, of course, I wouldn't have been there without him. He needed money for his pick-up truck and we'd made some real green at the end of that last trip. And now the Department of Fish and Game had called an emergency opening in a nearby lagoon, which excited even Woody, who rarely showed even the least bit of enthusiasm. It would be just twenty minutes; this was rare for salmon openings, which could often last up to a day or two, or even more. We'd have to be perfect.

"This could be *it*," he said. "Be ready boys."

We entered early in the morning at the peak of high tide, through a narrow opening that was barely a couple of boat lengths wide. It was a tricky maneuver. The rising ocean had turned the small channel into a surging whitewater river, with Woody doing his best to keep the *Lancer* between a rock wall and a long gravel spit. As crew all we could do is stand and watch, holding tight to the rail. Unfortunately, Woody over-corrected slightly to starboard and the hull suddenly scraped to an abrupt halt on the gravel beach, sending each of us tumbling to the deck. Getting to our feet we found ourselves suddenly breaching sideways in the current, water breaking against us amid-ship and the deck momentarily awash.

Our vessel tipped precariously to port and worst of all it was now blocking the way for the boats behind us. This may have been my first true Oh Shit Moment.

Fortunately, Woody acted quickly, positioning us with poles on the bow. After a perplexing maneuver of bursting full steam ahead, which seemingly pushed us further ashore, he adroitly placed the *Lancer* in full reverse, rudder hard to port, and with the current in his favor and the crew pushing for all we were worth, he dumped us backward into the lagoon. Looking down from his place on the fly bridge with an offhand smile, he shrugged.

"Guess we'll have to paint the bottom of the boat," he yelled.

Once we were settled and the tide had turned around, there were seven boats inside the lagoon. A handful of those unlucky souls who hadn't made the tide-change were circling out-side it and cursing their bad timing. Inside the lagoon, we were truly astounded—even the old timers commented on nature's bounty. There were sockeye salmon as far as the eye could see, rising like machine-gun fire across the surface of an otherwise mill-pond-calm lagoon. We watched in amazement as Woody's sonar screen went black with the clouds of schooling salmon that were amassed underneath the boat.

In a couple of hours a plane would land and a countdown would be initiated. After a skippers meeting, it was decided that rather than fight for position we'd surprise the Fish and Game officer by co-opping, each of us laying our gear in a calm, methodical, almost choreographed performance. And when the plane arrived, that's just what we did. Each boat moved calmly and succinctly to a preordained spot and laid out their gear; even our set was skillfully closed off and worked to perfection, like the pros we were.

Despite the nearly perfect parlay of our gear, almost immediately we knew something was wrong. Unlike the other boats around us, our circle of net began to shrink and too damn quickly. We looked at everyone else in dismay as they began listing under the bulk of the fish they had ensnared. I saw on Woody's face a pained expression, one of anguish shared by Mark and Ray. And I felt it too. How could it be that we were the only ones finished with absolutely nothing to contribute to the co-op? A water haul! It was almost unbearable, especially for the old man.

Sometime during the all-consuming task of hauling gear we heard the plane take off, and I saw Woody, still on the fly bridge, first looking at the other boats and then up toward the sky.

"Get ready, we're going to let her go." We all looked up in disbelief. "You heard me," he shouted. "We're going to make a set."

The twenty minutes allotted to us was long gone. The plane was certainly coming back, or maybe they were still around somewhere, watching us. Woody could lose his license or even go to jail. I suddenly knew why Woody was a legend, and it was for more than his status as a screamer.

"Let it go, goddamnit, *now!*" he shouted.

I waited a split second, in order to make eye contact with Mark and to be sure he had braced himself. Then I let it rip, sending him, our skiff, and our gear out on another run. I saw Mark scramble to the stern of the skiff, drop the motor and start it in one motion, and heard the jubilant hoots and shouts of encouragement from the other boats we were co-oping with, almost certainly looking on in amazement.

We'd gone with half our gear before closing it up—a short set—working feverishly and almost in a panic to secure the lines and pull the seine over the block. Only then, our gear half in the water, half on deck, did we begin to relax. We looked like everyone else hauling in fish. Maybe not like the highliners but we were somewhere respectably in the middle. And while our set may not have been the biggest, it was by all accounts the most daring and being part of it would likely be worth several beers at the bars back in town.

Add to this that we were one of the larger capacity boats, and after loading several smaller boats' fish into our hold, that's just where we were heading, back to town. And we would have a tidy sum to boot, some of which, Mark said, he was going to make sure we got.

• • •

We arrived exhausted and slept right there at the cannery dock. It was the first and only time I ever saw Woody crawl into his usually overlooked bunk. After we unloaded in the morning and before we returned to the slip, Mark broached the subject.

"I was going to get that truck today," he said, starting off a little sheepishly. "Remember, the one I was telling you about?"

"You know," said Woody, "just because we're in port, doesn't mean the work stops."

"I know that," replied Mark, "but the guy I'm buying it from, he's leaving town tomorrow. I've got to get the thing today. And I have to get some money from you." There was a sudden, sharp turn in Mark's tone. It wasn't threatening—even he wouldn't threaten Woody—but he wasn't asking either. If it had been me wanting money, I would have been flatly refused and told in no uncertain terms to wait like I was supposed to until the end of the season. But Mark spoke with a strength and conviction that someone like Woody responds to and even respects. It was something I would need to acquire if I were going to survive here, because Woody's was a world in which only strength begets fairness. One which the meek shall never inherit.

Luckily this time I was able to ride Mark's coattails all the way to the cannery office and another draw. This time we got $1,100 a piece. It was what Mark figured he'd need to get by. He'd pay a thousand bucks, half of what he owed for the truck and enough apparently to take possession of it. He'd settle the balance after our next trip. That would leave him a C-note for pocket money, and I'd have nearly a grand in the bank. Oh, how our fortunes had turned— and there was no telling how much more Woody still owed us.

Faye met us at the *Lancer's* slip. As Mark and I had worked and lived together, and had gotten to know each other, I began to pick up on why he and Faye might have been together. I hoped I was wrong, but I suspected Mark didn't do some things very well, like read, and I began to think he may have latched on to Faye because of her tendency to be somewhat motherly and her ability to help him navigate some of life's pitfalls.

Likely in her early fifties, she may have been a lot older than Mark, but she was younger than Woody and her presence tempered the old man, though she refused to step inside the cabin.

"Whew," she said wrinkling her nose. "What is that smell?"

"That, my dear," said Woody, inviting her in, "is the smell of money."

"I think I'll just wait out here for my husband, if you don't mind. Are you men almost done?"

"Are we?" asked Mark, assuring the old man that we'd be back whenever he needed us before turning my way. "C'mon, we'll buy you breakfast," he said, mercifully rescuing me from an afternoon swabbing the engine room or chipping paint.

I took my cue and made an exit before Woody had time to object. Neither Mark nor I had it in our minds to waste a sunny afternoon on the *Lancer*, or to return for at least a day or two. We'd both heard how Woody was notorious for losing deckhands every time he came to port, so no wonder he did everything he could to avoid coming in. Now he was probably worried we wouldn't be back, especially with a fresh draw on our pay. But with Faye there he held his tongue, waving as we left.

• • •

As I followed Mark and Faye, it was difficult to believe this world of boats was the same strange place I had so reluctantly entered only a little more than a month ago. Now, with a wad of bills bulging in my pocket, I was sauntering down the same dock as if I owned it. Past the pukers, the pleasure boaters, and past the tour boats with their lines of visitors gawking enviously, or at least we thought enviously, at the fishermen.

We continued up the ramp and to the nearest greasy spoon, the Breeze Inn. At this restaurant and bar, a perpetual steam-table of odors rose and mixed with the remnants of last night's stale beer and this morning's fresh coffee. The three of us pushed our way past a throng of tourists waiting to be seated and sidled into the bar. It was barely eleven o'clock, and despite the cleaning lady still taking care of last night's mess, there were a few of us in there. An old timer was sucking a Bloody Mary and a couple of fellow seadogs had just come in from the fishing grounds. It felt strangely liberating and slightly scandalous to be sipping a pre-omelet beer at that hour, with neither Mark nor I having showered for nearly two weeks and still clad in our work clothes and rubber boots. We didn't care. We were fishermen in from battling the sea and were entitled to laugh in the face of convention. We all liked the way it felt, including Faye—our conspicuous decadence, the way we fit in and stuck out at the same time, blending into the local color, the very thing that distinguished us from just about everyone sitting in the restaurant.

We told Faye all about the boat, how the old man never really slept, how happy we were—or at least I was—to have Ray join the crew, and about my falling overboard, my second Oh Shit Moment.

Just after finishing that legendary set, I had been giving the deck its usual quick wash-down as we headed to the other side of the lagoon. A small section of net had been stacked over the rear quarter deck, looking solid yet hanging precariously over the edge. One step—one thin errant step—was all it took and down I went. Three, four, five feet I fell before hitting the water and slipping beneath its frigid, silty, glacier-blue surface. It was like watching myself in slow motion as if from outside, air bubbles swarming around me, not fearing for my physical wellbeing at all. Strangely enough, I had been worried what Woody would say once I surfaced, which in a short time—even with layers of waterlogged clothing and heavy boots—I did. Mark had called to Woody the minute I went over, and the old man had already maneuvered the boat next to me. From my vantage point clinging to its side, the boat's confines, which usually seemed so stiflingly small, suddenly appeared enormous. Its black mass towered above me and my arms were too weak from hauling gear to even begin to hoist myself to safety. Still, I worried what Woody would think. I swore at my own carelessness and swung my fist in futility into the swirling water, perhaps hoping subconsciously that my anger might curtail Woody's. He did scream, but not at me. He screamed at Mark, directing him into the skiff and through every maneuver, every grueling effort of extracting me from the cold, incapacitating grip of the ocean.

"Go put some dry clothes on," Woody said once I was back on deck. There was not a trace of anger in his voice, only relief. And later, he actually poured *me* some coffee.

"Don't feel bad," he had said, as if I had passed a necessary initiation, "it's happened to everybody."

That night, however, it would happen again over and over. Only this time it was in the open water of the Gulf, out of sight of land and with no one to see me fall: left behind in the night, floating in the abyss, forgotten as the boat slipped further away, its running lights fading into the distance. Or it was the old anchor dream, my pant leg caught as I'm helplessly carried downward beneath the surface as I had been that afternoon. Only this time without any hope of returning.

• • •

After a hearty breakfast at The Breeze and several drinks, I returned with Mark and Faye to their friends' house—the small rented cottage on the edge of town where Faye had been staying. It felt strange after having been in a tent or on a boat for so long to be surrounded by knickknacks, to walk on carpet, to sit on a couch in front of a television, to take a real shower, and to actually use a flush toilet rather than sitting on the cold rail of the *Lancer*. It wouldn't be long, however, before the fatigue set in. Whether it was the strain of the previous two weeks, drinking beer for breakfast, or the sheer luxury of being in someone's living room and stretching out on a rich lawn of carpet after a long, hot shower, I didn't stand a chance. The soft swirl of voices faded and I allowed myself to succumb and fall into the throes of the deepest sleep.

When I finally woke up who knew how many hours later, I found only Mark, snoring soundly on the couch above me. Later we went to get his truck, which looked as though it hadn't been run in ages. The camper, fortunately, was in a little better shape; it had a few patches here and there but inside it was almost cozy, with a little table, nice cabinets, and a stove and refrigerator that Mark assured me were in working order.

"It's kind of small," he conceded, "for two people."

"Yeah," I agreed, "kind of like being on the *Lancer*."

I watched Mark's lips part in a wide grin. "Except without Woody."

"Well, you could always ask him to move in with you."

Mark all at once bent over in laughter. "That's right," he said between gasps.

I was surprised at how long it took him to recover so he could fill me in on the rest of his plan. Once he coaxed the dead truck back to life, which he somehow miraculously managed to do, I was to follow in my car closely behind the unregistered and unlicensed vehicle as it wheezed and sputtered through town. Then, hopefully, down a rough stretch of dirt road to Lowell Point, where some other friends had invited them to park it and where Faye would stay, living in the camper until the close of the season.

Later that evening, when I met up with my friends, who were actually done early for once at the cannery, I noticed something had changed. I'd seen it on the dock-workers' faces when we unloaded. Gone were the hearty smiles of new recruits, and after a month of sixteen-hour days, they were replaced by the dour grimaces and in some cases blank stares of weary veterans. Also apparently gone were the bonds of common experience. All anyone could talk about were plant politics and gossip, who was hooking up with whom, and why someone wasn't getting a certain job. A couple of times I even entertained the idea of returning to the *Lancer* and to my bunk where I had grown used to sleeping. While my friends had a whole army of workers back at the plant who knew what they were going through, I now had only Mark and Ray to commiserate with.

21

OH SHIT MOMENTS AND MIRACLES

ILIAMNA BAY, APRIL 1997

IT CAN BE kind of strange how guys out at sea attempt to occupy themselves, and I wonder if part of the lure, the excitement, is knowing what might happen. On one tender for example, we had watched time and again a recorded television special on the world's most dangerous jobs. It included a piece on crab fishing—likely a precursor to *Deadliest Catch*. Over and over again we had watched a large boat slowly being engulfed in waves, crewmen swept overboard and later abandoning the sinking vessel, hoping to be rescued by the Coast Guard helicopter that was likely the one filming the disaster. While the crew of the *Iliamna Bay* may not have been as blatant as those guys watching that crazy video, there were plenty of stories with plenty of Oh Shit Moments recounted as we whittled away the hours before being allowed to fish.

"Well, at least you learn from them," I said.

"You should," said Karl, "but I don't think that's always the case. It depends on the severity of it. When you get through something that's not that bad, it sometimes raises the bar of what even constitutes an Oh Shit Moment. Close calls can actually make you immune to danger."

I knew what he meant. It's like getting away with something, and then the next time it's kind of expected—you know you'll get away with it, you feel less intimidated.

"It's like that story of the frog that's in warm water," Karl said. "They turn the heat up little by little and he doesn't notice."

"Yeah," said Tim, "but you know what eventually happens to that frog."

"I didn't say it was necessarily good," replied Karl. "It's just the way it is."

I really wasn't sure. My Oh Shit Moments had mostly been quick—falling in when I knew I'd be picked up, traveling or hauling gear in bad weather—stuff everyone goes through, but nothing disastrous enough to put me off fishing.

"Well, it's likely a matter of degree," said Tim, who had by far the most experience and therefore far more Oh Shit Moments than the rest of us. "It definitely changes when it goes beyond an Oh Shit Moment and it becomes a 'Come to Jesus Moment.' I know we've all had some of those."

Karl mulled it over. "Really, in all the years I've been fishing, out of all the Oh Shit Moments, I've only had one go that far. It was setnetting. I should have known. None of the neighbors were fishing—that should have been a sign. We'd tied a skiff out on our gear and were heading in, in the other skiff, between tides. Had two of my sons and two deckhands. It was blowing forty knots and the surf on the beach where we were landing was really big. The motor quit. We got it started again but the thing died on our approach to the beach, in the breakers. I thought we were done for—somebody was going to get killed, maybe one of my boys. But one of the deckhands, he'd just been goofing around and had carved this giant oar out of a tree. It's like twelve feet long and this is the first time it's been in the skiff. We used that thing to keep the boat straight and somehow, miraculously, a big wave just deposited us on the beach. The boat swamped, but we were all okay. Afterwards, I just stood there and shook. Yeah, that went well beyond an Oh Shit Moment. The bar was lowered after that. It changed what I was even willing to do. Lesson learned. I've been a lot more cautious since that day."

"Well, it all adds up," said Tim. "You might not think it at the time and go about your business, but it accumulates. Even little things add to the wisdom . . . well, maybe not wisdom, but experience anyway."

I realized in that instant, as Tim began to describe his first seiner, the *Dutch Maid*, that one man's Oh Shit Moment might just be another's Come to Jesus Moment, or vice versa. Either way, one made you stronger—at least that's how it seemed to me—while the other might make you stop, make you hesitate. And for a guy like Tim those critical junctures—if he had time to think about them, engineer his way out of them—simply didn't constitute a Come to Jesus Moment, or at least what most of the rest of us might consider one.

"Yeah, that boat," he was saying, "it was an old wooden one, with white oak ribs. We hadn't had it long and we were on the other side of Cook Inlet when a storm hit—a pretty good one. Even in sheltered water there were three- or four-foot waves. We looked and through the fish hold you could actually see the planks separating."

"Holy shit," I said, picturing what was probably the last thing in the world you would want to see on your boat. "What did you do?"

"First, we borrowed a gas-powered pump from another boat, but it wasn't quite doing the trick, so we ended up bailing with five gallon buckets all night long, barely keeping up. We couldn't put it on the beach till morning, when we could see a good spot. When we did, we discovered a bunch of planks were rotten—really rotten, totally punky. We sent a pilot across to Homer, who brought back some sealant. We fastened the planks well enough to fish the next day and make it home. We fixed it up, replaced the bad planks, and I sold it at the end of the season. It fished ten more years over in Kodiak. When all this happened we thought we might lose the boat, but there were other boats around who knew what the situation was, so we weren't in fear for our lives. I really haven't had any near-death situations on any of my boats," he said, even though I knew he had been witness to some, including two crashes of spotter pilots—one in which he was first to the scene.

"Probably the worst happened aboard this boat," he said, almost pondering out loud, and immediately grabbing our full attention, if he didn't already have it. "We were coming across the Inlet. The boat was still fairly new to me, but I'd had it long enough to know it wasn't running quite right. I took a look out and the back deck was low, like underwater, and the seine was beginning to float. And we had our kids onboard; my youngest daughter was in the fifth grade at the time. I woke them up and got them into the skiff. In the meantime the net washes off, which helps, and I get the pumps going."

"Holy shit," I said again. "You must have been freaking out."

"No, once I figured out what was going on, I knew we'd be okay as long as the engine kept running. You see, there were vents on deck at the time—air intake to the lazarette. Kind of a design flaw."

"I'm guessing that's been changed," said Karl.

"Of course," Tim replied, "right away. Also, the high water alarm didn't go off. The fish hold was full at the time, and with that low deck and those vents flooding the back compartment . . . well, it was a miracle we didn't sink."

"Good thing you noticed it when you did."

"That's for sure." Tim said it matter-of-factly. "We dealt with it though. You make corrections, you learn from it, you go on."

As it so often does, talk of near misses led to general crazy fishing stories and I shared the one about that wild extra set in the lagoon with Woody. Despite all the crazy things these guys had seen and been through, they couldn't believe it.

"That's just plain nuts!" exclaimed Tim, and Karl, being a permit holder, agreed. "Who in the hell would do something like that?"

"That's nothing," I went on. "One time we made a set on a Sunday, in an area where we didn't have a permit."

"There's no way," Tim gasped. Karl looked on in disbelief.

"Oh, yeah," I said. "You wouldn't believe some of the stuff that went on aboard that boat."

22

ATTEMPTED PIRACY ON THE HIGH SEAS

LANCER, JULY 1984

WHEN IT STARTED off, I had planned on a leisurely day, settling in with the Sunday paper and a coffee. That's when I saw Mark's car approaching.

"Just tell Woody you couldn't find me," I told him when he suggested I go along. He said we'd scout for some fish, pull one of Woody's shrimp pots, and maybe try some sport fishing. It'll be fun, he assured me, a pleasure cruise. "Besides," he said, "the old man's seen me, and I don't want to go alone. You have to come."

"What about Ray?" I asked.

"That's just it. He's missing and Woody thinks we're going to jump ship too. He's sure Ray'll be back, but I think the old man just wants to keep tabs on us."

So there I was, heading east out of Resurrection Bay, in the opposite direction of where we usually fished. At least it was sunny and calm, and the doom that always accompanied us seemed less intense, maybe because we were just going for a boat ride, supposedly. And by mid-afternoon, anchored in a secluded cove, sunning myself on deck, I almost believed it. But with my head nodding, and drifting on the verge of actual comfort—something rarely experienced on the *Lancer*—I began to hear the calm water break all around me. At first it was just a few scattered splashes, which quickly crested into pandemonium.

"What in the hell . . . ?" Woody emerged from the cabin, eyes groggy and looking out of place without his cap, bald head glaring in the sun.

"Fish," called Mark from the fly bridge.

"Goddamnit," cried Woody, "they're all over the place. Humpies." Pink salmon, everywhere, as far as the eye could see—the ocean literally going black with them. Pinks, or humpies, are the smaller more oily cousin of the sockeye, and were worth only about a quarter a pound to the sockeye's dollar. Still, that would be about ten grand if the *Lancer* were full of them. I had no idea of the ramifications of what we were about to do, it being Sunday and for all intents and purposes we were fishing without a permit.

"Let's go," said Woody, all at once. "Clear the deck, get the skiff ready."

Ignorance was a flimsy veil and would never stand up in court, nor would the excuse that I was just following orders like some fishy lackey of Hermann Goring. Still guilty in the eyes of the law, and rightfully so. Nevertheless, I watched as Mark set out in the skiff and my pleasure cruise, my afternoon of leisure, went to hell—as I should have known it would.

It started off easy enough, closing off our circle of gear as we'd done repeatedly over the last several weeks. However, when Mark handed his end of the seine off to me, there was no one to hand off the leadline to or to gather the web in between. The tide had begun to turn and the wind had come up—only slightly, but enough to push us slowly toward shore. We were like a sports team with a man down and pitted against the elements. With Woody taking over Ray's job, we were temporarily stranded without a helmsman and a consortium of wind and water was conspiring against us, swinging the boat and blowing one end of the seine underneath us. Adding to the confusion was a swarming mass of ten thousand fish seething inside, placing an incredible force on the whole set up—net, boat, and skiff. Then, in a single moment, the net tightened up, the block squealed in protest, corks dangled in midair, and the *Lancer* all at once tilted to one side against the strain of the net and its unlawful bounty. Woody could no longer contain himself.

"Goddamnit," he screamed through clenched teeth, cursing not only me and Mark but the fates, the Karmic forces of nature that now threatened to topple us. With Mark back on board we all pulled hopelessly at the gear. Irretrievably stuck, we would have no choice but to cast one end of the seine loose, releasing our ill-gotten gain, and patiently wait for the incoming tide to free our net. This fiasco consumed the very last of my free afternoon. Waiting for the tide, Woody's anger turned sullen and Mark dejected, and all of us would have a lot of explaining to do if the wrong person happened to sail or fly by.

When the net did finally come back on board it was damaged beyond immediate repair, needing to be replaced when we reached town. That left me still on the *Lancer* at midnight, hauling the new seine on board. At least we hadn't wound up behind bars.

23

FISH, BEARS, WHISKEY, AND
THE DEAL OF A LIFETIME

RAY HAVING TURNED up, there was no doubt I would be going back out to finish up the season. It wouldn't be more than two or three more trips, four or five weeks tops. In the meantime I had learned extremely valuable lessons: that I indeed did possess a strong constitution and a rather steep threshold for pain, and that I could survive a fairly high degree of mental anguish. Frankly, I had the ability to stick out just about anything—a trait that would serve me well far into the future. I'd also found that if I actually asked the right question at the right time, Woody would give me a reasonable answer. I even mustered up the nerve to ask him if there might be some way he could possibly wake us other than by jolting us out of bed by cranking up the engine. Much to my surprise, Mark and Ray both chimed in to adamantly back up my request. After that, Woody would call down in an overly sweet and uncharacteristic tone. "Oh boys," he might chant in a singsong voice, "it's time to get up. Pretty please, boys, time to rise, there's fish to catch." And as we dressed we'd often hear him grumble. "Goddamnit," he'd say to himself, "is this a fishing boat or a goddamn cruise line?" Then he'd call down to us, "I suppose you want your coffee in bed or help getting dressed."

Mark and I might give each other a knowing grin, even laugh a little, but only Ray would have the guts or the familiarity to answer. "Yeah, that'd be good," he'd say wearily, sometimes even in a rather surly tone, "get down here and bring that coffee when you come."

I knew there was nothing to be afraid of. Sure, Woody had been a boxer and had seen his share of barroom altercations, but the guy was ancient. Still, despite his advanced years, that toughness was something I'd never want to put to the test. Hell, even Mark gave the man his space.

I imagine that underneath that crotchety exterior though, the cantankerous old bastard likely had a sense of humor. It was a wry, warped sense of humor, to be sure. And perhaps because I was so reticent or because it was so often at my expense, I just didn't pick up on it at the time.

At least the screaming had fallen off somewhat as we learned our jobs, or maybe we'd just gotten used to it. Still, we always knew who was in charge and his barrage of comments always reinforced it. "It looks like a damn library out here. There's work to be done," he snapped at Mark and me, as we were waiting for him on deck before that third trip. Mark was flipping through a magazine and I was perched on top of our pile of corks, working my way through *A Farewell to Arms*. "Smartest goddamned crew in the fleet," he scowled. "If only you were smart enough to catch some fish."

Another time he demanded I "get that communist off this boat," when he saw I had also brought a Steinbeck collection aboard.

I glared at him in disbelief.

"You heard what I said. I don't want that communist on my boat."

Later, when I couldn't find the collection I was sure he had thrown it overboard. Still, I tentatively asked where it had gone, not sure what I would actually do when he said he'd tossed it. Would I leave, quit, throw something of his overboard? Then what, run?

"Oh, here," he said, retrieving it from the little hammock above his bunk.

"Were you reading this?" I asked.

"Of course I was reading it, goddamnit, what do you think I was doing with it?"

"Really?" I asked, astounded at what I was hearing.

"'Tortilla Flat.' My favorite story."

We stared at each other. I was dumbfounded.

"It's based on King Arthur and Camelot, did you know that?"

"I guess so," I said.

"You know, the knights of the Round Table—Arthurian legend. I love that goddamned stuff, have loved it since I was a kid. Besides," he said, "that story reminds me of a lot of people I used to know."

• • •

The fish were still plentiful and during the next couple of trips our routine had actually begun to fall into line. But life on any boat tends to be good—even on a boat like the *Lancer*—when you're making some money. The number of sets we were making was still high, though a good portion of them did contain fish, yet as the season wore on they came to be the less valuable pink and chum salmon.

During a rare break one afternoon, we watched as a black bear dug on the beach not far from where we were anchored.

"Wow, look at that guy," I said.

"That's one you have to watch out for," Woody commented.

"Why, how do you know?" asked Mark.

"Well, age," he said, after thinking about it a minute. "That's a young one—teenager in bear years, or maybe a little older, probably not gone from his mama very long. They're the dumb ones. Just like people, they're the ones think they know everything, do crazy stuff. Actually, it's them and the really old ones you have to watch out for."

Later that evening Mark and I had decided we needed to get off the boat and "take Mr. Sanchez for a walk."

"Here," Mark whispered, reaching into his duffel bag with a narrow wink of the eye. "Put this in that big coat of yours."

Contraband. Mark had smuggled and concealed it aboard, waiting for just the right moment to unveil his surprise. Together we smiled like mischievous schoolboys. Something as ordinary as a fifth of Canadian whiskey took on enormous proportions. It may have been a slice of everyday life on shore, taken up without thought, but out here it was priceless.

We landed the skiff a few hundred yards away. The *Lancer*, hanging on her chain, rigging captured against the vast panorama of mountain and forest, appeared like a picture postcard in which, from this distance, waterfalls were suspended and birds appeared held in mid-flight.

Finally cut loose, Mr. Sanchez ran with abandon, chasing seabirds and gulls with the same exuberance we felt upon being freed for a few hours from the rigors of boat life. Ah, to be free from the anguish of shared space, lifted from the bonds of indentured servitude, to breathe, walk, and speak without restraint. And the clandestine nature of it all, breaking one of Woody's steadfast rules, made it that much more exciting—every bit as intoxicating as the treat we were about to indulge in. We walked down the beach and out of sight of the *Lancer*, to a spot where long ago someone had enjoyed a campfire, their abandoned ring of rocks stood as an old calling card left by kayakers or fishermen. Mark had thought of everything and produced a couple of plastic cups as I laid down my coat, placing it to rest on the beach with the utmost care. I don't know what happened—there must have been a weak spot in the whiskey bottle or it touched in just the right fashion, because all at once the placid air of fresh spruce and sea-salt was overcome by the fumes of disaster. There was suddenly the unmistakable musk of distilled barley malt rising and slowly beginning to register on our olfactory senses.

As I held up the coat, Mark and I watched in dismay as the whiskey streamed through its lining and out the corner, trickling onto the dry beach. Thinking quickly, Mark placed a cup underneath to catch what he could through the sieve of a ten-year-old coat and its foul, synthetic lining. We laughed at how hard up we'd become and tried to convince ourselves that the liquor would kill whatever soiled those pockets, before drinking a hearty toast to our liberty. Who cared what Woody would say when we returned with the whiskey-soaked coat, smelling as if we'd been to a distillery? What could he do, fire us?

A couple of hours later we pulled the skiff alongside the *Lancer* and climbed aboard like a couple of highschoolers coming home late, snickering to ourselves as we heard Woody and Ray discussing the old days over a cup of joe at the galley table. I tried unsuccessfully to pass the old coat off to Mark before finally entering, walking through the cabin so nonchalant it was obvious, stopping in front of the cold stares of Woody and Ray.

"You guys smell pretty good," commented the old man.

"I don't know what you're talking about," replied Mark.

"You can't hide a smell like that from this old nose," he said.

That's when Mark gave in and began to laugh, recounting our whole hapless misadventure just like one of Ray's old stories—except this had occurred just an hour before. We all got a good laugh out of it.

"That's what you get," said the old man, "for not sharing with your shipmates."

The thought had never occurred to me, drinking with Woody. . . .

• • •

The spilled whiskey was perhaps the last of the few laughs we would share aboard the *Lancer*. By August the boat had grown increasingly small. I'd find out later in my career that it can happen regardless of a boat's size and often coincides with poor fishing and less money. With an increase in water hauls, bumping into Ray on deck or running face first into Mark's dirty socks seemed to reach its intolerable limit. On top of that, as the days churned into weeks and the jumpers became scarce, Woody continued to speculate. While the few other boats that had stuck around seemed to pick and choose where they might set, only laying out their gear if they were sure to mop up some of the remaining fish, we continued christening gear seemingly without thought, until it was more an act of desperation than any serious strategy. To make matters worse, Ray had turned glum and taciturn, grumbling at each set, and Mark had run out of smokes, making him downright unpleasant to be around.

Mark had never minded the hard work, but with each water haul he'd sneer and complain to me, "That's it, I'm done. This is bullshit." We all knew the end of the season was near and were just waiting for the old man to give in and call it. Finally, one morning Mark had enough. He walked up to him, demanding he radio for a plane.

"Okay," was Woody's only reply, the crooked half-smile on his face hardly disguising his displeasure, especially at Mark's insolence, but he could see we were all finished and if Mark left, even Ray wouldn't be far behind. We immediately dropped anchor and Woody cooked a big breakfast before heading to town, just like he had that first morning of the season.

Simple as that, it was over. Once we reached Seward, we would spend several days on final clean-up, Woody insisting that we wait until the cannery settled with him before getting our final pay. And I would have to head back to the campground.

It was mid-August and things were winding down at the cannery as well. The days there were cut to merely six or eight hours, which left ample time for hiking and parties. The workers were waiting for management to "call bonus," signaling it was time for those that wanted to quit to receive their end-of-season bonus check and return to their real lives. For those that wanted to stay or who called Seward home, work would trickle on for a few more months.

I wasn't sure just what to do. Mark had found another boat with a mellow skipper, he assured me, for halibut season. The season would last a mere twenty-four hours, and with the added prep and clean-up it would be a week tops, for which we'd make thousands. He'd also begun talking about partnering. "I've been looking into it, us getting into the fishin' game. There are all kinds of permits—set-netting, trolling, halibut—still easy to get. You and I could do that. Get our own operation." It sounded exciting. But I had only a semester of school to finish, and now that I was off the boat and having met some of the cannery girls, the hormones that had remained dormant or were scared off by Woody kicked back in, and with a vengeance. Unfortunately, it was all too clear that no one was available—at least not for me. The cannery girls had either hooked up long ago or were downright sick of all the attention and were ready to leave.

"I'll find you someone," Mark assured me. He'd tried before. Between trips, he and Faye had attempted to initiate something for me at a party, where I was one of the many and she one of the few. Danny was a little older, probably in her mid to late-twenties, and not bad looking; in fact, at the time she looked damn good, with brown, shoulder-length hair and a great body. I'd never seen anyone like her. She worked on a crabber as cook and deck-hand, chewed tobacco, sported tattoos long before they were chic, and swore like a trucker . . . or like a fisherman. And she was thoroughly enjoying being the belle of the ball, with at least half a dozen other guys vying for her attention. I'd see her later, at one of the end-of-season parties—one of many usually impromptu gatherings around a campfire—but after Faye went to bed that night Danny ended up with Mark.

Nevertheless, I entertained serious thoughts of staying. Despite the old man's ass-chewings and our hardscrabble existence at the campground, I had gained something important, or was on the way to, and realized now that I was free to enjoy it, that I loved this place. There was something barely perceptible—a rare and distant freedom that had all but evaporated elsewhere still clinging to life here. And I'd only gotten a small taste of it. I really hadn't even begun to discover Alaska's true essence: its bold, unrefined luster, its curious allure. It was huge, this place, not only in a geographical sense but a metaphysical one as well. And if I wanted to get to know it—including the part that resided in me—it would take some time.

The only thing left to do was call and break the news to my long-tormented mother. I'd have to tell her once again that I'd be putting my education on hold, this time to test my mettle here in the northland on the halibut grounds. It wouldn't be pleasant—not only because of the tempestuous relationship we shared, but because it was a call I'd made before, taking off for other, less consequential adventures. Over the years I'd been tempered somewhat to withstand at least a modicum of guilt, learned to even tune out some of what was being said. Yet what I couldn't ignore this time was the sharpness in her voice, far beyond anything I had ever experienced before. It was an overriding hurt, as if I were maliciously attempting to inflict pain on this woman who had done everything in her power to raise me properly—to see that I had clothes, a roof over my head, and most importantly a good education. If that wasn't enough, I was reminded of every seemingly selfish turn I'd made, of every activity I'd ever quit, as if college were the same as Little League or the Cub Scouts. I was told in no uncertain terms that it was about time I started acting responsibly. But what exactly was irresponsible about choosing Alaska as my destination or taking on the challenge of working on a fishing boat?

I held my ground and was offered a deal—a deal of a lifetime. My mother was often difficult to tolerate, but she always kept her word and stuck to her promises. And this offer included a future completely free of guilt and admonition—I could do whatever or go wherever I wanted, head back to Alaska if I so chose—if I'd only agree to return and finish that last semester. Her pleading, finishing the last of my desultory education, a lifetime pass on guilt and its accompanying condemnation—they were all good arguments for returning but hardly what stemmed the tide.

No, it came from somewhere completely different, emphasized perhaps by the cold shoulder bestowed upon me by a couple of cannery princesses and a hard-drinking crab queen. Returning to college would have very little to do with finishing my education and everything to do with the possibility of courtship and carnal pleasure. I would be heading back to where the ratio was much more in my favor and I held the hope of possibly luring a girlfriend to Alaska. Then I would come back and find Mark and Faye. Maybe they'd have scoped out some land by then and I could help them build a cabin, maybe even build one of my own on their land.

I was almost relieved to have made a decision, and only eight or nine days before I had to start the drive back. My college buddy Moo had opted to follow a girl to Colorado, and Dave and Peggy would be flying back, but I had picked up three other potential riders from the cannery. I just needed to get paid. Unfortunately, Woody and Ray had taken off to tender for a small jitney raking up the final remnants of salmon in a cove east of town. At least with Mark around and out of money, I knew I would eventually get paid. We had received over two thousand dollars in draws, yet I had no idea how much was left and realized that Mark, despite having apparently gone over Woody's ledgers, had no idea either. He'd simply been putting on a show. Still, he guaranteed me it was more than we'd already received—at least a few thousand. I lent him a couple hundred to get by. Unlike the beginning of the summer, however, money flowed. No one came by empty-handed and it was only the best in beer as well as big burgers and steaks. Mark and I had even put up twenty to thirty silver salmon in a friend's freezer. And soon we'd have all the bear meat we could eat.

Mark and Faye had been seeing its tracks around the camper, heard it had broken into nearby sheds and destroyed bird feeders. They even thought they'd spied its shadow on occasion, lurking through the woods. But then, early one morning, Faye literally met up with the beast face to face. She came out just before dawn to relieve herself and, still half asleep, turned around to find him standing there, a three- or four-year-old black bear within arm's reach. "He was right there behind me," she told me, still full of emotion later that afternoon, when I'd arrived to find his carcass strung up by its hind legs, ready to be butchered. "I could smell him, his fur, even his breath—he was that close."

Mark described her reaction as kind of a soft, high-pitched squeal, something so strange and off-putting that it immediately roused him from bed. Emerging with loaded rifle in hand and seeing the black bear next to his wife, he carefully took aim and dropped it with one shot. That one fateful pull of the trigger would alter his life, and perhaps mine, forever.

• • •

I helped skin and butcher the bear, aided by several cannery workers who had become regulars at their place. During this time we enjoyed a great many feasts of bear ribs and roasts slathered in barbecue sauce and accompanied by salmon, all the while waiting for Woody and checking the dock daily, hoping we might get paid. Mark helped me change the shocks and tune up my car for the trip east, which with four drivers we hoped to make in record time. When bonus was called the old man was still out, and with my carpoolers threatening to mutiny, I didn't know what to do. If we didn't hit the road soon there'd be no point in going.

Finally, with just days left, I saw that the *Lancer* had returned and I went to find Woody. My first stop was his old clapboard house, which looked like something out of "Tortilla Flat" or better yet *Cannery Row*, with years of accumulated old fishing gear and crab pots kicking around the yard. I nervously approached his door and knocked. It was with panic—because of course time was dwindling—and relief—because who in the hell would want to confront Woody—that I turned to leave when no one answered. I continued my search in frustration.

I did finally spot him, his mottled white cap and crooked gait, ambling down Main Street, unmistakable even from behind. After rather impatiently explaining the situation and that I had to get on the road, he laughed. "I really don't care what you got going," he said. There was a finality in his voice—the same voice he used on deck—that was impossible to argue or reason with. "I haven't had time to settle with the cannery, even figure out what they owe me, and until I get mine you're not getting yours. That's just the way it is."

I immediately went to see Mark. He'd take care of this. "We'll give him a day or two," he reasoned, "then we'll both go see him." His voice was calm and confident, but all at once had that menacing quality it took on now and then—something I usually tried to overlook. Today though, I was happy to hear it and to have it on my side, and in this case to hopefully get us what was rightfully ours.

• • •

It was Sunday, the car was packed high with gear and my riders were waiting. It was the last possible day I could leave. Mark and I negotiated the maze of old fishing equipment and engine parts lying around Woody's yard. I thought he knocked rather tentatively, yet when the old man answered, there was no question Mark meant business.

The old man just kind of gazed at us through his half-open screen door.

"We need our money," said Mark, abrupt and to the point.

"I told him," said Woody, glaring at me, "it just doesn't work that way. The cannery doesn't even know what they're getting for the fish, so they haven't settled on a final price for the fishermen. I haven't gotten any money, and when I do, that's when you get yours."

"Look, we both need some money," demanded Mark, explaining again that I'd be leaving, and that if Woody could at least give us some or most of what he owed us we could settle the difference later.

It seemed like the conversation went on for a long while, never really reaching the point of argument, but had the same tenor, the same underlying tension, as if it could escalate at anytime into something ugly.

Finally the old man relented. "Okay, I'll give you what I think I might owe you," he said.

"I've got a good idea what that is," said Mark, even though he hadn't the slightest notion.

"C'mon, let's go," said the old man, all at once seemingly free of malice. He even escorted us to the Alaska Shop, a variety store on the main drag where we could each cash the smaller of two checks—money to tide Mark over and to send me on my way. That check was for five hundred dollars and the manager assured me that since it was from Woody, he would have no problem cashing it. The other check was for $3,950. We might have been getting short-changed, but I hardly cared. It was a fortune—more money than I'd ever had at once and it came just in time.

"Do you have enough in the safe to cash his other check?" asked Woody.

"I'm not sure if I want to drive across the country with all this money," I protested.

"You might want to cash it if you can," replied Woody, "or I just might forget who you are and stop payment on it."

I paused and looked at him. Did he mean that, or was he taking one last shot at me? Maybe because I was free now or perhaps because I was still feeling empowered with Mark by my side, I spoke freely. "I won't forget you," I said. "Goddamnit, Woody, I know where you live and I'm coming back."

He glowered at me momentarily before beginning to chuckle. "You've come a long way, kid," he said, shaking my hand. "You be careful with all that money."

I also said goodbye to Mark and Faye that evening. "We'll be somewhere around here," said Mark. "We'll scout things out a little more. Maybe when you get back we can figure something out, maybe look into that fishing operation."

"You bet," I said shaking his hand, hugging Faye goodbye, totally expecting to find them living the Alaska dream—now our mutual dream—when I returned in May. I had no idea it would be the last time I'd see either of them.

24

THE GOODS ARE ODD

"**S**o your Mom got you to return to school, eh? Probably good you went back and finished up." That was Karl, always sounding like he wanted to be a teacher.

"Yeah, it was good," I admitted.

"I had no choice there," said Karl. "I had to finish school, but the folks were not pleased when I came back to Alaska the second time, only twenty years old, in an old beater pickup, and Cindy and I weren't married. I had to promise I'd get insurance for the both of us before we left, or my mom would never speak to me again."

I told Karl about the deal I'd made with my mother.

"That's perfect," he said, having a good laugh over it. "You can't go wrong with that. Did she stick to it?"

"I have to say, she did. And just like you I talked my girlfriend, Mary—my ex-wife now—into coming back up with me. In a pickup. But a nice one, that I'd saved all winter for."

"Good move there."

"What, the truck or the girlfriend?"

"Both," said Karl.

"It was tough back then." I turned, explaining the situation to Brad. "There weren't many women around."

"I'll bet," he said. "How long were you married?"

"Not very long, but we were together, on and off, for ten or twelve years."

"That's too bad," he said, "that you broke up."

"It happens a lot up here," said Karl.

"Not for you," I replied. "Getting together so young, you know, you either grow much closer or much farther apart it seems, and I guess we grew apart." I still hoped though, that there was a situation for me out there, something like what Karl had or what Tim had found in Peggy, his second wife, who seemed to share in everything. She had been with him on a lot of voyages and had even been the skiff operator on the *Iliamna Bay* before Karl.

"Things are better now, I gather," said Brad, "on the woman front, number-wise. Anchorage is actually about even, I hear, maybe even more women than men."

"You know what they say, though—the women—don't you?" asked Karl.

"No," responded Brad. "What?"

I could guess what was coming.

"You know, that the odds of finding a man in Alaska are good . . ." as he paused, I joined him in this common refrain, "but the goods are odd."

Brad, as most men do upon hearing this, just smiled.

"Regardless of how odd I am or the numbers, it was difficult," I continued. "After so long with one person, it was like waking from a date coma."

"That's what it would be like for me," laughed Karl.

"Well, think about it. I went from a college town, where you could be any drunk fool at a party and still go home with someone, and awoke a dozen years later, in my thirties, with women who are suddenly very picky. Worst of all, being out of circulation for so long, I had no idea—absolutely no idea—how to act."

"Wow," said Brad, "that is tough."

"It's getting better," I shrugged.

"Probably good you had someone for a while though, isn't it," he asked.

"Oh yeah. There were no divorce lawyers, we're still friends. It's all good. We just weren't ready. Both looking for something, going off on different adventures. She went off to mush dogs during the winter and I did my thing. But having someone to come here with to get things rolling was good," I said. "The whole time, when I was finishing school, all I could think of was getting back up here. I was working two jobs so I could buy a nice truck to bring with us. And I was much more prepared than the first time, with a little stash of money, a nice vehicle. The truck even had a cap that we could sleep under. Of course, you were well established by then," I said to Karl.

"Yeah, that was a few years before we bought our own fish sites, but we were done with school, married by then, and thinking about a family. That was about the time Tim was messing around with the *Dutch Maid*."

"I ended up working in the cannery that year."

"You went from fishing to the cannery? How'd that happen?"

"Yeah," I said, "kind of strange. Sometimes I do things a little ass-backwards."

Tired of shouting, competing with the clamor of the engine, I decided to leave it at that.

25

AN UNWELCOME TRUTH

SEWARD, JUNE 1985

ARRIVING IN **S**EWARD this time I was ready. The new truck had performed admirably and Mary and I had several hundred dollars between the two of us. I had thought of finding a boat, but a season with Woody had left me a little scarred. Quite frankly, I was also a little worried about leaving my girlfriend to the wolves on shore. I even considered the possibility of working for Woody again, if that's what Mark was doing. My main goal was to find him. He was what had gotten me through. I was sure he'd be around and we'd likely be working together. Maybe when we were out fishing Faye could even look after Mary a little.

My first stop was the *Lancer*. I was surprised to find Ray on deck in raingear, almost as if I'd just left him.

"Hey, look what the cat dragged in," he called to Woody, who emerged from the cabin, sporting his white cap and a long scowl on his face. He informed me they'd been fishing for cod. I got the feeling that he, and even Ray for that matter, seemed none too happy to see me. Maybe it was the way Mark and I had strong-armed Woody for our money; he'd had all winter to bitch to Ray about it and maybe that had turned him against me too.

"Just came to say hello," I said rather sheepishly, realizing at that point I wouldn't be working on the *Lancer*. "I just got to town. Have you seen Mark anywhere?"

"Mark, who worked on this boat?" asked the old man.

"Yeah, have you seen him around?"

"Hell, he's long gone. Flown the coop," said Woody, as if it were ancient history. Then he paused and gave Ray a kind of amused look, but not as if something was funny, just curious—as if he were interested in what my response might be. "He took off. On the run from the police."

"What? What did he do?"

"Well, I guess he shot a bear."

"Yeah, I know. I was here for that."

"He didn't turn in the hide and skull. You're supposed to if you shoot one."

"They arrested him for that?" I couldn't believe this.

"Guess he was wanted for something else too. Had a big to-do with his wife—beat her up or something. That's what I heard anyway. He took off, but before he did he busts her out of the shelter here in town, and they tried to run."

"So they're on the lam somewhere?"

"No, cops got 'em. He's in jail somewhere—that's where he is. It's not the first time I had a felon on the boat either."

I stood there dumbfounded, silence all around. This was completely unexpected, and I could feel them, through my dismay, staring at me for what seemed a long while. I didn't know what to say.

"Well," I finally muttered. "I guess I'll get going. I'll see you guys."

"Yeah, you be sure to stay in touch," the old man said as he turned to step inside, his sarcasm a final blow to what was becoming a very unwelcome return.

Immediately I went in search of someone who might know more. I sought out some of the people Mark and Faye had stayed with and others around town who knew them, but with the way things happen so fast in Alaska, for many it really was like ancient history. "Oh, let me think about it," they'd say, still eager after the long winter to share the story, yet there was no telling how out of proportion it had been blown by then. While the gossip varied, it seemed Mark had initially been taken in and questioned about the bear and his bail posted by the couple they'd stayed with before buying the camper. According to all accounts, sometime before fleeing, Mark had apparently struck Faye, who ended up in a local shelter for battered women. After breaking her out, they hit the road, forfeiting the bail their friend had posted. They were arrested a couple of weeks later. As to what he'd been wanted for, the stories varied, though many said they were sure it was murder or at least questioning in a murder case back in Michigan. I don't know why, but I didn't want to know what he'd really done. We'd grown close during our time together and I knew—knew for sure—he had a conscience. But I could still picture it—something violent inside, driven by temper, and I thought it better to leave it as it was. Since the consensus was that he was in jail in another state and locked away for a long while, there was nothing I could do now. And rather than knowing an unkind truth I preferred to know nothing at all.

26

THE ONSET OF SWS
AND THE LARGER WHOLE

SUMMER IN A cannery is no summer at all, and it didn't help that my first one in the cannery was accompanied by some of the nicest weather on record. It was nearly round-the-clock work, broken up only by a six-hour sleep break. Between sleep we all lived for respites of a mere fifteen minutes, called every two to two and a half hours. Emerging from the dank bowels of the cannery I'd find Mary, who worked as hard as anyone I'd ever seen, first alongside me on the "slime line," scraping with a wide-bladed knife the bellies of pink and chum salmon, and later in the "egg room," packing caviar for export. Together on breaks, we would soak up just a little bit of the precious warmth of the sun and steal a glimpse of the outside world. We'd discuss with other workers our ailments—perpetually cramped legs and repetitive motion injuries. The Safety Manager treated these by doling out wrist- and leg-braces with abandon and Advil by the bucketful.

I was often greatly vexed and envious at seeing the boats tied up out front. I would watch them unloading at the dock, their crews laughing together. I would spend the next several years, as I worked my way through the ranks at the cannery, wishing that I could join them, longing for a new start and a return to the sea; if only I could get over my lingering fear—the certainty that I would encounter another Woody.

What I did discover was that most of those who stick it out at the cannery have some sort of plan, to sustain them—even something simple. They have set a goal for themselves, perhaps making enough money for school or to travel, or to buy land or build a house. Those that don't have something to drive them succumb quickly; those who do stick it out gather strength from their shared suffering. It was our dream—or mine anyway—to own a little piece of Alaska. The only question was where. Alaska is such a big state. But time was in large supply or so it seemed, and there was so much to discover and learn. With my mother's blessing, and for the first time in my life free of school, I felt I could finally unfold my young wings. And what better place to take flight than a state not only as physically large and diverse as Alaska, but one that seemed at the time to welcome those seeking answers, or at least an alternative.

However, it was during this time—after my first season at the cannery and during my first winter in Alaska—that I began experiencing the symptoms of Seasonal Work Syndrome, or SWS. After enduring a series of 100-hour workweeks I found it was not only okay in rural Alaska to be unemployed and collecting unemployment checks, it was expected. In the state office they not only told you how to apply, but how to maintain and extend your benefits, and never made you feel even the slightest twinge of guilt about receiving them. Of course, there was still the nagging internal strife of not having a real job—of not climbing the corporate ladder or pursuing a title. After all, it was difficult to discard a lifetime of admonitions, such as "idle hands are the devil's tools," but it was also enlightening to learn that there was actually another way we might live.

I do remember, however, being told by a couple of old sourdoughs that having time on your hands is easier when you're young. Of course, I didn't believe them. That's when it still passes slowly, they said, and you feel like you have all of it you will ever need. Enjoy it, they insisted, because that's when, at least in other people's eyes, you're given some leeway and cut some slack to sow your wild oats. Unlike later, they warned, when you're apt to be viewed as something of a bum.

I passed their warnings off as merely the sourness of old sour-doughs, who maybe hadn't accomplished all they'd set out to. After all, I did have all the time in the world. And with that I allowed myself to continue to succumb, to fall—if it can be seen as a fall—into SWS. I was enabled in this by taking a position as a caretaker for the National Park Service. Only about eleven miles from Seward, with just a footbridge across the Resurrection River, Exit Glacier—part of Kenai Fjords National Park—was then difficult to reach in winter and was accessible only by snow-machine, dogsled, or skis. While today there are tours and snow-machine rentals, during my stay it was still largely untouched. Weeks would pass without my even seeing another person; my most frequent company were the moose, coyotes, and wolverines.

Back then, I already sensed a future where Mary and I would grow apart. She had taken off to mush dogs, while my six months in residence were planned as somewhat of a spiritual retreat and what I saw as a second, more complete education. It was all part of a great adventure in a truly wild place and with the added bonus of having what seemed to me very plush accommodations. Though I had only an outhouse and kerosene lamps, my very well-built and -appointed cabin came with a fully stocked kitchen and the large living area had picture windows that bestowed an unsur-passed mountain view. It was a view that for sheer magnificence would have competed with any the Alps or Himalayas had to offer. And the limited duties—keeping the roofs clear of snow, regular ski patrols to the bridge, and observing and noting the movements of the resident mountain goat population—accomplished with a high-powered spotting scope, usually while sipping coffee in front of the wood stove in my living room—left the bulk of most days open for me to pursue my studies. I began rising well before dawn to compose my "coming of age" novel, the one I'd heard all writers need to get out of their system, but which should be subsequently incinerated in order to spare the rest of society.

It may have been a vain act, a seemingly futile effort, but it was part of a larger process, a larger whole, and best of all in an environment completely out of view and thus out of range of judgment. I was in a completely safe place, where commonly held notions had become trivial, had no meaning, and could be, at least for a time, cast aside. No one was there to steer me from my course or make me doubt myself. Taking my cue from the likes of Joseph Campbell during the Great Depression, where due to the lack of any meaningful work he was granted the freedom to pursue a wide range of subjects, I began my quest. Never before, even in school—especially in school—had I the liberty of reading so many books at once and on very divergent subjects: from poetry to classical literature, natural history to metaphysics to religious theory, and all at my own pace. When I tired of the life history of mountain goats I would turn to Byron or Keats, then jump into some Jack London and move on to Descartes before finishing the night out with a little something on meditation or perhaps a short story. All the while I fought to stay awake, to prolong to the very end another glorious day, though I would often succumb by seven or eight in the evening—long after the winter sun's early retreat. Rising again by three or four the next morning, I was anxious to begin it all anew, an education like I'd never experienced. Combined with a healthy diet and plenty of exercise, I was in the best shape spiritually and physically that I ever had been and I found myself wanting to prolong it. This made my quest to own a cabin retreat where I might live simply and at least somewhat in this fashion even more keen.

27

CRUISING TO THE SOUND (OF THE ENGINE)

ILIAMNA BAY, APRIL 1997

WE'D ALL MENTALLY prepared for it. Usually the most arduous and likely dangerous situation for a seiner is crossing the Bering Sea. But as Tim said to Peggy via the marine operator, we'd been blessed with good weather and calm seas—the best conditions that he'd seen in all his years heading out west. As we cruised steadily farther and gained on our destination, we did begin to pick up a swell, along with slightly onerous radio reports hinting that an opening might indeed be called at anytime. At this Tim began pushing the *Iliamna Bay* even harder, placing a dramatic strain on the engine. Still, a good twenty-four hours away, there was not much more we could do but keep plugging ahead, hope the engine continued chugging, and—as so much of fishing is—simply pass the time.

"So," said Brad as we cruised, "you didn't go back out fishing after the *Lancer*?"

"No, not right away. That summer spent with Woody was tough, and with nothing positive to compare it to, the longer I stayed on shore the worse it looked. The thought of getting stuck in a similar situation left me kind of cold," I said, and frankly without someone like Mark there to bolster me, I didn't see how I'd go back.

"I'd also settled in at the cannery," I continued. "It had gotten a lot easier as I moved up into better jobs. I still had a large part of the winter off to travel and after a couple of seasons was making pretty good wages."

"Yeah," said Brad, "but at a cannery, aren't you just kind of a cog, a nameless face?"

"That's for sure," I said, after thinking about it for a minute. "A small cog in a giant operation. Even if you learn a lot of jobs to replace various cogs, that's just it—you're still easily replaceable."

After a couple of years it was also becoming unbearably stifling. Every day watching the sea, seeing the boats come and go, the salt air nagged at me, reminding me I'd left something important behind. I belonged somewhere else. I hadn't realized until after a few years at the cannery how shell-shocked Woody had left me or how much I had relied on Mark. That's when a likely compromise presented itself. I could go out on the fishing grounds as a buyer. It would mean a cut in pay, but I could spend time on boats, while still being employed by the company. As a representative of the cannery, and with my boss on shore, there was very little potential for experiencing another skipper's wrath. Sure, I was expected to pitch in with daily chores. And once onboard, after they were confident in my abilities, they might even rotate me into wheel watch, but I was still a representative of the company and often treated more like a guest than a crewman.

It was during this period that I began to see that there were basically two types of people who signed on to go commercial fishing: those that weren't capable of doing anything else and those who just couldn't do anything else. For these, it was in their blood. They had to be on the water. A couple months on the herring grounds aboard various tenders reminded me that there was also a variety of skippers to contend with, from obliging and polite to downright crazy. And deckhands as well—something I would have to deal with soon enough.

At last I had begun to feel comfortable on the water again, even to the point of considering a return. I knew I just needed to find the right situation. That's about the time one of those circumstances the north country is famous for—one of those opportunities just overheard in passing—somehow presented itself. I'd heard that a local couple with three young children were in need of a second deckhand at their setnet site in Prince William Sound. A family operation. Just what I needed to overcome my reluctance. *The perfect remedy*, I thought, as I set out to meet the patriarch of this fishing family and convince him to hire me.

I would find Bob Linville working at a shop in town, literally up to his elbows in fiberglass, repairing a large skiff. It was difficult to know what to make of him—his tall, lanky frame, the way he talked, just blurting out whatever he felt like. He was about ten years my senior and seemed amiable enough, but I almost didn't take the job because of the way he downplayed his fishing prowess. He kept saying how they'd had a good season last year, but he didn't want to get my hopes up. "No telling how this season's going to be," he went on. But he offered up a high percentage: fifteen percent off the top, plus a bonus for staying the whole season. The living conditions also sounded interesting, fishing out of skiffs and spending nights on shore in cabins that the Forest Service required to be dismantled in the fall and re-set each spring. A lot of work, he said, but part of a comfortable lifestyle. And that's just what it was: a lifestyle. That's what got me. You had to love the outdoors, the wilderness. You had to want to be there, he explained, be part of the family, enjoy the place—not just come out for the money.

We would set out a few weeks later to the Sound, just Bob and me, to begin setting up for the season. Once we were done, while the kids finished school and Patty, Bob's wife, closed up their house in town, I'd have a few weeks off. During this time Bob would head out to Cordova to fish the Copper River in his drift boat. After my time off, I would meet the family and our other deckhand at the Whittier harbor—about a thirty-five mile boat ride from our site.

As Bob and I took off from Seward on our way to set up, I was happy to be out on the ocean again, and as always found myself mesmerized by the sharp features of the outer coast. Later, I was taken by the sublime beauty of the cove at the head of Main Bay, where the family had chosen to make their camp. Setting up with just the two of us was a bit of a challenge, but it was the kind of work we both found gratifying, as we could see the immediate result of our labors: watching the cabins come together, attaching the roofs to each one, seeing our pile of firewood grow. As we fell into the rhythm of work, time passed quickly. I could see that Bob worked hard, expected a lot, and spoke his mind. He constantly bantered about politics—state politics, world politics, fish politics—but it was difficult to decide where he stood. He often tipped the scale either wildly liberal or conservative, depending upon the issue or how he happened to be feeling at the moment. One thing for certain, he was sure of himself and his abilities, but at the same time also seemed to want to encourage me. As I began to get to know him, it appeared that in many ways he shared similar traits—the positive traits—with both Mark and Woody. He possessed the know-how and confidence of the old man and offered the rather rough support proffered by someone like Mark. It was also a work situation that seemed like it might share many similarities with my time at Exit Glacier, and I actually found myself looking forward to it, guardedly optimistic about the future. But I had yet to meet our other deckhand. Perhaps Bob had forgotten to mention to him that part about wanting the lifestyle and not just being there for the money.

• • •

"You ever think of buying into that fishery, out in Main Bay?" Brad asked, forcing me back from the edge of memory, out of that warehouse of the mind I so often found myself pushed into by the infernal surge of the diesel.

"Kind of a long way out there," announced Karl, looking up from one of his crossword puzzles.

"That's what's good about it," I responded. "Living out there, being able to go explore. But if I was going to buy in I'd buy a drift permit and boat. You don't need to worry about hiring much of a crew, maybe just one other person, and you can move around. Now, if I had a family it would be a different story."

"Setnetting is the family fishery," said Karl.

"The setnet fishery in the Sound's a very different type of fishery compared to what Karl's doing, isn't it?" asked Brad.

"Biggest difference is you don't have the big tides like these guys do in Cook Inlet, so you don't just pick your nets between tide changes, you work them all the time," I said. "Also, in the Sound we have just a couple nets, 150 fathoms of total gear—so one big net, maybe one hundred fathoms long and another net fifty fathoms, and they have to be attached to shore, not anchored out all over the place like the Inlet."

"It's also clear water," Tim chimed in.

"Yeah," I said, "so you have to constantly wash your nets. We have pumps in our skiffs that shoot water out in a concentrated spray at one spot over the rail of the boat, and as one guy pulls along the net the other waves the webbing through the spray, cleaning off jellyfish and algae."

"Are the jellies bad?" asked Brad. "I hate those bastards."

"Oh, man," I replied, "you have no idea. You have it easy on a seiner."

"It can't be that much worse."

"Oh, it is," I exclaimed. "The jellyfish fly. I've had stings every-where. I mean *everywhere*. You touch something, even long after you wash your face or take a shower, and it transfers the spores. I've had 'em on my tongue, in my eyes. Some guys wear welding masks out there when they clean the gear. Worst sting I ever got though was around my neck. It just happened to land there and as I moved, the collar of my shirt and raingear aggravated it to the point I couldn't stand it. I was going crazy. Only time I had to quit fishing and go to shore."

Tim laughed, in commiseration rather than sport. I'm sure over his long career he'd had all sorts of stings, ailments, and injuries he'd fished through. "I've heard of the Linvilles," he said a little while later, "they do pretty well, don't they?"

"It's funny, I've been fishing with them for seven or eight years now and they don't think of themselves that way, but they've definitely been highliners for a while."

"It's a long season out there, isn't it?" asked Karl.

"I guess so. At least a couple months, mid-June to prep and well into August, but it goes fast."

"So when you're not out there, what are you doing?" asked Brad.

"I've tendered a few times for herring," I said. I'd already told him that, more than once, but maybe he hadn't heard over the din of the engine, or maybe it was Karl or Tim I'd told. It was getting difficult to remember by now, taking watch at all hours, sleeping at strange intervals, the way time elapsed—the days lengthening and just melding together. We were losing all perspective of minute, hour, day, or week. "I also worked for the Department of Fish and Game on a couple of projects, running boats and stuff."

"And the coffee shop," added Karl.

"Yeah, and the coffee shop, but that's only when I run out of money."

"Good thing they keep taking you back," he said.

"I guess so," I snorted. "But what I really love? I love being out in the Sound. It really is amazing, you guys know that. I've made a lot of money out there too, at the setnet site, more than some permit holders, but it sure started out rough."

28

THE DECKHAND FROM HELL

PRINCE WILLIAM SOUND, JUNE 1990

PERHAPS IT WAS a sign of getting older, but it seemed a bit more difficult to drop something comfortable, like my job with the cannery, in mid-course and change tracks. But I'd done it so many times in the past, why should it have been difficult all of a sudden, especially with such high hopes? Even though I had purchased that cabin in the woods and was saddled with land payments, I was sure I was doing the right thing, quitting my somewhat regular employment and setting out for Whittier, not down to my final dollar yet, but knowing I would be by the time fishing began.

As I pulled up to the harbor I saw Bob's boat, the *Coyote*. And there were Patty and the kids, whom I'd met back in town. They were just starting to unload an entire summer's worth of supplies from their vehicles and onto the small vessel. The kids, Annie, Gus, and Bobby, ranged in age from seven to three and were rambunctious and tow-headed. They would have looked at home in some sort of Norman Rockwell wilderness print. Bob and Patty, on the other hand, would not quite have belonged. Far taller than most and decked out in rubber boots and Stormy-Seas coats, they were pure hard work and toughness, and lacked that Rockwell innocence their kids still possessed.

I spied our other deckhand, who was far from tall—especially next to Bob and Patty—but carried himself as if he were, walking with chin held high as he lugged a box down the dock.

As I approached, Bob stopped to introduce us. In age, Jackie fit somewhere between me and Bob. He was from Australia, by way of Missouri, where he now lived with his American girlfriend. All I knew was that he'd worked on a tender last season that serviced Main Bay and that Bob had hired him a few months before me. I had no reason to think he'd be anything but amicable, despite his crushing handshake or the way he suggested we stop lollygagging and get back to work. But it wouldn't take long. Soon enough I'd find I had fallen into another sticky situation and it was far too late to get out of it.

At the family's insistence, I had brought Foster along, the most affable Newfoundland/Husky mix and my near-constant companion for the past several years. He'd keep the Linville's dog company. "Besides," said Bob, "it's a good place for a dog." But Jackie thought otherwise, telling me that in Australia they keep them outside, where my dog never slept unless we were camping. He'd be pressing me to do the same. Another immediate point of contention was the wood stove in the cabin we shared. He'd fire it up with the door wide open and leave it that way; more than occasionally sparks would spit out onto the plywood floor. Despite the fact that Bob insisted we just work it out, I had to draw a line somewhere. I insisted that Foster sleep in the bed I made for him on *my* side of the cabin, and that he shut the fucking door of the wood stove before the place burned down, and with us in it.

The plan once fishing started was for Jackie and me to work together through the early season. The gear we used in the Sound were long nylon gill nets, stretched between a cork- and lead-line and designed to ensnare the salmon by their gills when they inadvertently swam into them. In order for that to happen, the netting must be nearly invisible to the fish, and thus the reason for its constant cleaning. To accomplish this Jackie and I would have to spend countless hours together working the gear. During this time Bob would fish various openings around the sound in the *Coyote*, returning between fishing periods to spend time with the family.

During the peak of the run they had arranged for the teenage son of one of their friends to join us. He would watch the kids while the four of us, Bob and Patty in one skiff, and Jackie and I in the other, would pick fish.

But the sense that there'd be trouble had begun almost as soon as we left the dock. "We're here to work not have a holiday," Jackie said when he saw my sport fishing equipment and heard me asking Bob about hiking. He told me to be prepared to stay up all night during openings, that we'd put in twenty-four or thirty-six hours straight if we had to. Whatever it took, he said.

I tried to make the best of it, defer to him when possible, but couldn't help wondering, of all the fishermen in the world, all the crew they might have hired, how could I have wound up with the Woody of deckhands after all these years? Still, despite the fact that Jackie liked to take control and that this guy seemed to possess all the confidence I lacked, there were finer points that needed clarifying—like occasionally when he was about to steer the skiff full-throttle into a rock pile.

"You don't tell a man how to drive, mate," he'd scream over the whine of the outboard. And when I grabbed the tiller once, purely as a reaction and to avoid possibly being injured, that really set him off. The next time it happened I simply stated the obvious, that we were heading for rocks, and when he didn't change course I braced myself for impact and watched as he hit the floor. No need to say a thing. I just stood there, basking in satisfaction and hoped the boat was still watertight. I would let him explain to Bob why there was a big chunk missing out of the skeg of the motor.

29

WHAT GIVES?

ILIAMNA BAY, APRIL 1997

"**W**E'VE HAD GUYS like that," said Karl, one afternoon, after I'd told him about Jackie. "Well, maybe not that bad," he said on second thought.

"I sure have." Tim turned around from his place at the wheel, his face suddenly animated. "I could write a book about some of the deckhands I've had over the years. One guy was actually stealing from us—from our house. Had a drug problem he had supposedly recovered from."

"Apparently not," said Karl.

"Definitely not," replied Tim. "Another guy I left in Whittier got drunk and stole a forklift and ran it into a car."

"Yeah, I haven't had anyone like that," repeated Karl. "They have to be able to live with the family, and I've got a pretty good radar for assholes."

"Bob didn't," I said.

"Is that why he hired you?" Karl jibed.

I raised my hands in dismay, realizing I'd stepped in it as soon as he spoke. "Maybe so," I admitted. "But this guy, Jackie, worked on a tender the year before—he knew how much the Linvilles made. I found out later the skipper of the tender advised Bob not to hire the guy."

"What did he do it for?" asked Tim.

"Well, Bob probably never saw it, him being an asshole. Jackie was always cracking jokes or messing around with the kids. Had to be the center of attention."

"It can be tough," admitted Tim, "you always think you're a good judge of character, but you never know. I can't tell you how many crew members I've had who've acted like they absolutely hate every minute of it and then come January or February they call and say how much they loved it and want to come back . . . it's difficult to fathom."

"Listening to you guys, maybe I've done pretty well," said Karl. "But I've had a couple of lazy guys. Had one, no one else would work with by the end of the season, so he was in my skiff."

"How come you didn't fire him?" asked Tim.

"Friend of a friend, you know. That kind of thing."

"I've been there," acknowledged Tim.

"Well, that wasn't Jackie's problem," I interjected. "He wanted to work, or at least said he did, but when Bob was gone fishing somewhere else and we'd have a thirty-six-hour opener he'd want to stay up all night. This was before many fish were coming in. I'm all for working hard, but after the net's clean, what do you do, sit around in the dark and pick the occasional fish that wanders in?"

"It's a setnet," said Tim. "And out where you guys are you're not picking between tides, so it's out there fishing with or without you. You'll just burn yourself out staying up all that time if there isn't anything to do."

"Exactly," I said. "We wouldn't have caught any more fish or made any more money by staying up, or I would gladly have done it."

"It's a long season too," added Karl, "and there's a difference between just working and working smart."

"Well, this guy didn't even want to go in when Patty would come out and tell us she had made dinner. And we're two minutes from the beach. He'd speak for both of us, like he was in charge, and I'd say, 'no we've been out for four or six hours, I'm going to eat.' Then he'd mope, like he was losing money or something the whole time we were on the beach."

"It makes absolutely no sense," said Karl.

"I talked to Bob about it when he was there between openings, but his response was something like, 'You guys need to work this out for yourselves.' He just wanted things to go as planned, he didn't want to have to be ordering us around all the time."

"What about staying up all night? Did you work that out?"

"I told him I was going to bed for a few hours and he said, 'suit yourself, *mate*. I'm going to work.'" I told them this, trying out my best Australian accent.

"So, anyway," I continued, "I get up in the morning and he's in bed and I can't get him up. We have someone watching the kids by then so Patty and I go out to the nets and one of the skiffs is tied to the set and it looks like a ghost ship or something, it's scary. The boat's dirty, with seaweed and jellyfish everywhere, an oar is broken completely in two, the cover is off the pump and strewn on the floor, a gas tank is overturned. It's dead calm, been calm all night. So I don't know—looks like maybe he had a tantrum or something, like maybe he couldn't get the pump started or wash the net by himself . . . which, I admit would be pretty difficult. But Patty and I can't believe it. We just stand there for a long time looking at each other and going, 'wow, what the hell, this is really weird.'"

"Probably didn't do him a bit of good either, being up all night," said Tim.

"Didn't do any of us any good. He didn't even deliver any fish. And fishing was open until six or eight that night and he didn't get out of bed until four or five. At least he helped us pull the gear. We don't say anything about the skiff or that he slept all fuckin' day, but I'm sure Bob heard about it when he came back. By the next opener it's to the point where we're working alone, each in our own skiff. And that was fine with me."

"But that's dangerous," commented Tim.

"That's exactly what Bob said when he came in. By this time I told him I was ready to leave."

"What did he say to that?"

"He begged me to stay—at least through the big push of sockeyes. I'd made a deal and didn't want to let him down, and I needed the money. But it was getting to be unbearable. Also—I don't think Jackie was being really mean to my dog, like hitting him—but he wasn't being very nice to Foster, the way he talked to him or acted around him." After all, at that time Foster seemed like my only friend. "It was also the way he wanted to work the nets, he just didn't do things logically, which made it more effort than it needed to be. At one point he tells me that in Australia if two guys aren't getting along they go outside and settle it with fisticuffs or like men, or something like that."

"So, did you take it outside?" asked Karl.

"Well, he probably would have kicked my ass. He was the one that was mad. I was never really mad at the guy, just fed up. I'd tried everything to get along with him, to be nice to him."

"So what did you say," asked Karl, "about going outside?"

"I said this was America and we have guns and if it came to that I'd pop a cap in his ass. I think I actually said that, *pop a cap in his ass*."

There was laughter. This was hardly something you'd normally hear aboard the *Iliamna Bay*, nor was it something any of us, especially me, would say. "If I remember right he probably laughed, too," I said, "but just a little, because he wasn't really sure if I was serious or not. Which was good. He probably knew I'd about reached my breaking point."

"So, did he ever shape up?" asked Brad, coming out from his bunk down below. He was bleary-eyed and looked as if he'd just woken up but must have been able to hear the conversation as we shouted over the rumble of the engine.

"I think Bob, even though it had taken him nearly half the summer, finally saw what was going on and laid the law down to Jackie. Told him we couldn't be in separate skiffs and if we didn't start getting along one of us would be going and it wouldn't be me."

"Did that help?" asked Karl

"It did. But his animosity kind of shifted to Bob after that. It sucked that he was being kind of pissy toward Bob. But for some reason he started being nice to me. We started working the gear together and in a way that made more sense, he loosened up a little—even went sport fishing with me a couple times."

"So it all worked out?" Brad asked.

"Oh no. It got a lot worse from there." They all turned to look at me.

"Well, you see Bob has a difficult time making up his mind sometimes, especially about little things, and, honestly, it can be hard to deal with. But not really for me, I kind of go with it," I said. It was difficult to explain, but the cannery had given me staying power and having worked for Woody, I had the patience to deal with Bob and his vagaries. "But that kind of thing, changing your mind, it's tough for other guys," I continued, "and fishing in other parts of the sound had slowed a little and Bob was starting to be around camp more. Also, he had apparently mentioned at some point that there could be a lull or they might shut the season down and that there was a chance Jackie could go back to Missouri for a visit."

"In the middle of the season?" asked Tim incredulously.

"Yeah, I know, but I guess the year before it had been shut down."

"I'd never let someone go during the middle of the season," said Tim.

"Bob warned him about leaving with things still open, but it was slow and we weren't making money, so Jackie left for two weeks."

Tim nodded, his nod accompanied by a knowing smile.

"You know what happened, don't you?"

"The fish came in."

"Oh yeah," I said, "with a vengeance. I was making $3000 an opener, with two openers a week for the two weeks he was gone, and when he got back you know what happened?"

"Let me guess," said Tim. "The fish stopped."

"Yup. The reds did anyway, but the humpies were just starting."

Then Tim burst into full-blown laughter. "At what, twenty cents a pound?"

"Might not have been even that much."

"And after what, two dollars a pound for reds?" asked Tim.

"At least," I said.

"That must have really set him off," replied Tim.

"When he came back I avoided it as long as possible. He'd been so hepped up about making all this money at the beginning of the season, I didn't want to be the one to tell him. I didn't know what he would do."

"If someone like that, any crew, is in it only for the money," he said, "you don't want them. They're just not going to last."

"And they make it miserable for everyone else," commented Karl.

"That's it," I said. "When he was gone I saw what a good time it could be, even though we worked our asses off." It was true, without Jackie, even though we'd likely lost money being shy a deckhand, everyone had begun to relax between and even during openings.

When I'd talked to Bob earlier in the season and told him I might be leaving, I'd also said I didn't think setnetting was for me, that I might not be cut out for it. It wasn't the hard work, I explained, it was the mystery of how this whole particular operation worked. My discontent derived not only from having to deal with Jackie, but perhaps was also an offshoot of my past with Woody, not understanding the workings of his boat and being constantly taken to task for it. Part of the problem was also the past several years, falling into the malaise and repetition at the cannery, only to come here and find my boss was the consummate technician. He'd studied electrical engineering and appeared to have a very analytical mind. The site at the mouth of the bay had been thought by many to be unfishable. But Bob had devised what at first seemed to me a mysterious system of anchors and lines to hold the gear. They also made our largest net—six hundred feet long—zig and zag in "hooks" with little rooms and corners of net which would confuse and subsequently trap the fish. It was ingenious, a mind-blowing feat of engineering, and although my brain worked on a very different plane than Bob's, I had finally begun to see it. And now that we were working together, just Bob and me, I had also begun to see that under his tutelage I might actually be able to do this and do it well, and it made me reconsider leaving.

"So what happened, when that guy got back and found out about all the fish you caught?" asked Tim.

"Well, I tried everything to avoid telling him, saying we'd done all right, that I wasn't exactly sure, but he knew. Eventually he asked me point blank, so what could I do, I had to say."

"What did he do, blow up?"

"No, not on the outside. That's just it, he was quiet, sullen. You could see it in his face, though—the way it wrinkled up, his mouth crinkling at the corners, and you just knew it was ripping him apart on the inside."

"Serves him right," one of the guys muttered and they all agreed. But even at the time I couldn't help feeling a little sorry for him. I'd never seen anyone so completely defeated. Maybe because he needed an ally, he continued to grow steadily nicer to me, even as his resentment toward Bob grew. For some reason he blamed Bob for his bad fortune and lost income. On top of that, as it often does in the coastal rainforest, a large low-pressure system, with its dark skies and perpetual showers, had descended upon us, making work even more of a grind. Also, the smaller and less lucrative pink salmon or humpies were now flooding into the bay. With the influx of salmon, Fish and Game had extended the openings to a couple forty-eight-hour periods per week, and we were left picking endless nets of fish for a few hundred dollars a day each rather than a few thousand. It was decent money, but the fact that he'd lost 12,000 dollars—more than half the season's wages—continued to gnaw at him. As we lay in our bunks, hands swollen from hours and days of picking humpies, listening to the measured crest of raindrops build and ebb against the plastic roof of our cabin, he told me time and again that he couldn't believe it. His anger and discontentment built up with each passing day. Soon it was difficult to wake him up at all, and Bob and Patty would ask where he was as we ate breakfast. I'd tell them about attempting to rouse him and try to explain that I wasn't his boss and I couldn't very well be expected to order the man out of bed. Then each morning, after Bob finally got him up, the three of us would set off in a skiff together, in silence, often in a downpour. I'd stand between the two, separating them like a human buffer, trying with little success to bridge the gap and endlessly attempting to spark any kind of conversation at all. Jackie—someone who had been so loquacious at the beginning of the season—would remain desperately quiet for the entire day, day upon day. Something would have to give.

30

PLAYING THE ODDS

MAYBE THINGS HAD been going too well. We'd seemingly had such good luck, a considerate crew that worked together so well, a big payday in Cook Inlet, and splendid weather for our crossing of the Bering Sea. But with our late arrival, had our luck finally taken its inevitable turn for the worse?

Tim had been running the engine nearly full bore for almost twenty-four hours. As we entered Togiak Bay, news broke over the airwaves that the fleet had been put on "twenty-minute notice," signaling an opening was imminent. It came with the usual scuttlebutt, the excited calls, and the last-minute planning that always accompanies the desperate plunge into a herring roundup. We fielded calls from our pilot and the other boats, requesting our location as we called out frantically, attempting to locate the tender that carried our seine. We were hoping, probably beyond hope, that we might somehow load it aboard and be ready to fish, but the closer we came, the more the realization crept in: nearly six days of travel, and if we'd arrived an hour earlier, if we'd only hurried our refueling on the Aleutians or not paused somewhere to check the engine and give our ears a break, we'd be out there now with our partners circling a school of herring. It could almost be read in Tim's eyes, seen in the way he held himself at the wheel, his stance settling from tenseness into a posture not really relaxed but simply loose, urgency briefly succumbing to anger before finally falling into stubborn acceptance. Oh, he'd still try, but we all knew there was just no way we were going to make it.

Still, there always remains that slight ray of hope. The tender that carried our net was not far away—in Kulukak Bay taking herring from gillnetters. The gillnetters, many of whom were locals fishing from small skiffs, had been open all day. Because this tender was assigned to them rather than a seiner, they were stationary, and this bought us a little bit of time. We'd already unchained our skiff and prepared the boom to lower it into the water as we pulled alongside the other boat. Seiners would not be fishing immediately adjacent to us, but the sea was alive with vessels and the sky suddenly became a tapestry crisscrossed with weaving aircraft. As we placed buoys between us and fastened the two boats side by side, we heard it, first broadcast in unison from outside speakers on each of our decks and then echoed across the water from various vessels—a ripple effect of bad news reaching us in increments. It was the announcement that fishing was open and the final acknowledgement that there was no way we'd have our seine unpackaged, loaded, and ready to fish by the time the twenty-minute seine opener was over.

We all slowed down and for a minute just watched the madness commencing around us—without us.

"Damn," muttered Karl, expressing a feeling of utter helplessness in a single syllable. We all felt it. There was the chance—however unlikely—that the boats could fill the entire season's quota during those twenty minutes, and we'd have come all this way for nothing; we'd have to turn back around and start the long voyage home. We continued without urgency to unload the seine from the hold of the tender onto its deck; then we dragged it across the rails of both boats and onto the deck of the *Iliamna Bay* in the anticipation that we would need it.

When we were finished, we found a resting place on the east side of the bay inside Anchor Point. Finally we were free from the constant drubbing of the engine; there was complete quiet broken only by the modest hum of the generator. At last, after nearly a week, we pulled the small foam plugs from our ears and took our first long walks on the rocky beaches of Bristol Bay.

Awaiting the official report, Tim was likely more anxious than the rest of us. Apparently our partners had not fared well. This was perhaps a sign that no one had and that there might be another opener or maybe two. I was relieved, especially because Tim had insisted, not being here in time, that we wouldn't be part of the co-op for this opener. Thankfully Tim's argument that we not share in the catch, an argument made against his crew's wishes and the other skippers' insistence, was rendered moot by the poor catch and the report broadcast that evening by the Department. Like our partners' catches, most of the herring had been "green" and unsalable and so were released back to the sea. Apparently our luck was still with us and we still believed in it and the inevitability that we'd hit it big this next opening.

So, here we were again reciting the fisherman's refrain of "hurry up and wait". We whiled away a good part of a precipitation-and fog-filled week raingear-clad walking the beaches or squirreled away in our bunks reading. Occasionally we'd raft up with our partners the *Rafferty* and the *Sea Mist* so the skippers could talk.

Butch Schollenberg, skipper of the *Sea Mist*, had been fishing practically his whole life. As a kid he'd gillnetted with his father on Cook Inlet, and bought his first boat in 1976—just two years after graduating from high school. Greg Gabriel had done just about the same, starting on a beach site with relatives when he was thirteen, running a setnet skiff during breaks from school; he had graduated only a few years following Butch and bought his first boat soon after. The two now ran their own salmon seiners in Prince William Sound: this was the second year Greg had joined Butch's crew for herring. Though they were only in their early forties, they had a lifetime of fishing experience between them, which included innumerable Oh Shit Moments.

Like the other skippers, Grant Henderson of the *Rafferty* was experienced and had fished his entire life, but to me he seemed a bit different than the others. He was slightly more high-strung and seemed a tad younger than the skippers in our group, though on second glance probably wasn't. He just carried himself that way. Like Tim he kept clean-shaven, but he seemed more professorial than the others, reminding me of someone I could have taken a class from in college rather than an Alaskan boat captain. Like Tim he was rather meticulous, but he was also a bit of a contradiction. He suffered from motion sickness but loved boats and had his pilot's license. He claimed to be cautious and unlikely to take chances—and he appeared that way—but had also seen more Oh Shit Moments than just about anyone out there.

The skippers' chats usually took place aboard the *Sea Mist*, the largest of the three vessels, but could easily spring up just about anywhere. That was probably around the first time I heard Tim say that he had made a pact with himself never again to set past Usik Spit—which meant out past Bristol Bay proper and close to the invisible demarcation that signals the edge of the often turbulent Bering Sea. I asked him why and he was a little vague at first, saying it was just a nasty place to fish. "It's unpredictable," he said later. "Scares a lot of guys off. It's definitely not a place for beginners. The pilots though, they like it—there's not a lot of competition and it's a good place to pick up a lot of fish . . . a good place to lose them too." Come to find out Tim had done more than lost fish out there, he'd twice ripped his gear, once completely in half, and he'd witnessed more than a few boats roll in the erratic currents. "No," he said. "There's no way we're going out there."

With the constant wet weather, the deckhands tended to keep to their own vessels. Each night we'd listen to the reports from test fishing. The herring reached ripeness and maturity in a matter of days—though it seemed slow to us—and as the week wore on the fleet went from twenty-four hour notice to six, and then finally to one. At last we were going to have a shot at these fish. But as it turned out, the fog was as thick as chowder and the ceiling low—we likely wouldn't have the help of our spotter plane.

Earlier that morning, however, I had entered the cabin to hear Tim urging our pilot, Brad Heil, over the radio to please play it safe and stay grounded like most of the other planes. But Brad thought he could get airborne and since there weren't many planes in the sky, he easily ducked in and out, above and below the clouds, and after a couple hours in the air—with Tim shaking his head in both dismay and appreciation—he reported a possible spotting of several small schools of herring. They were spread out over the area and there was only one extremely large school. Unfortunately, it was just inside Usik Spit, on the edge of what Tim referred to as the danger zone.

The herring were congregated in a fairly tight ball, and it was determined by the skippers that just one boat should risk itself on what could very likely turn out to be—as it always was in this area—a dicey but very profitable operation. I don't know how it was decided that Tim would make the set, but I suspected—even after what he'd said and the pact he'd made with himself—he'd volunteered. My guess was that he just couldn't stand to be the one *not* fishing, the one standing by, because, after all, he was a fisherman. And fishing was what he did and that's what he had to do.

31

THE CYCLE OF LIFE

MAIN BAY, JULY AND AUGUST 1990

I **HAD TO ADMIT** that while I would have much preferred everyone to get along, if Jackie had to be sour at someone I was glad it was Bob rather than me. It was much easier being his confederate than his enemy. It made for a better living situation, yet it made the long, dragging days drag even longer and even the good days of fishing were barely tolerable. And Bob wasn't about to address the problem. He was hardly one to form a focus group or, for that matter, even try to mediate an awkward situation. So, in the middle of an opening, on what turned out to be one of our few sunny afternoons, he abruptly let go of the gear, pushed the skiff free, and started the motor and without a word we headed toward the beach. Neither Jackie nor I knew what was up. It didn't look like he had jellyfish in his eyes. It was uncharacteristic of him not to at least announce that we might be taking a break or headed in for coffee, to take a dump, eat lunch—something.

As usual, the outboard motor drowned out even the slightest possibility of conversation, which by this time had fallen far below what was cursory. I looked at Jackie and he just shrugged before turning ahead to watch the approaching beach come into view. Here, our other skiff and the *Coyote* were moored and the kids—after several days stuck indoors—were outside enjoying the first nice weather in nearly a week. As Bob nosed the boat onto the beach and cut the outboard, I jumped out to pull it up. That's when he finally spoke.

"Go pack your stuff," he barked at Jackie, "I'm taking you to town." As usual his voice was booming and abrupt—a trait that to the uninitiated might be taken for anger—but today was not any louder and perhaps even more subdued than was the norm. I just stood there and watched. Jackie and I were both for an instant stunned, pushed even further into the prevailing silence. While it should have been obvious this was coming, it took us both by surprise—especially Jackie.

Immediately, figuring this was none of my business and something I should best steer clear of, I retreated toward the Linville's cabin. Patty was there, waiting on the small porch. As I approached one of the kids was about to run to the boat and I quickly stopped him. "You better come with me," I said.

"I think he's gone," I told Patty when I arrived and she asked what was going on.

It was impossible not to watch, and from the distance we could see the conversation escalate, growing animated and more heated— at least on Bob's side. But we were only able to pick up bits and pieces of what transpired. All the while, Patty tried to explain to the kids that it was just a discussion and not a fight. That's what she was hoping, at least. But with these two, how could we be sure? I couldn't imagine Jackie would think of fisticuffs or trying to settle this like a man. Bob was twice his size and twice as angry. "You don't want to be here," I heard him say, "you don't talk, you're pissed off all the time."

It looked like Jackie tried to deny it, but even across the beach his cheeks were flush, and it was obvious the man was about to give in to emotion—perhaps tears rather than anger. I realized then that despite his behavior, this had come as even more of a shock to him than either of us had initially thought. I heard him say, "Yes, I do respect you and your family." It looked as if he were backing down a little, trying to explain himself, but I was sure Bob had made up his mind and that there was no turning back. Jackie was going to be run off.

Patty and I were thankful to see Jackie finally proffer a hand before heading to the cabin to pack, and even more thankful when Bob reluctantly took it. I really didn't want to see Jackie, but wasn't sure where to go. I didn't really want to be around Bob either, so I was relieved when he went to prep the *Coyote* to get it ready for the ride to Whittier. Before he left, he asked Patty and me to finish the opener, which would conclude that evening. This gave me the welcome opportunity of hanging out and having some lunch with her and the kids as she prepared herself to tend the nets.

I waited until Jackie was ready to board the *Coyote* and helped him haul his gear to the boat. Once we were alone, he said he was glad he was leaving. I offered my commiseration, saying I was sorry this had to happen and he actually said it was nice meeting me and wished me luck, shaking my hand as well.

With Jackie gone and the fishing extended to five days a week we began to slide into an easy and steady, though somewhat tedious system. Even Bob grew visibly weary of picking humpies and we would set out later and later each morning, the long days and conversation in the skiff straying far afield as we attempted to whittle away the day. Despite the fact that we could both be rather somber, some silliness did accompany our serious discussions and debates as we freely wandered into subjects ranging from the personal to the political, from ideology to belief to sentiment to feeling. I found that being thrust together for long periods allows people— especially willing participants anxious to pass the time—the latitude and liberty of letting their guard down, exposing various sides of themselves while at the same time seeing those of the person they share this space with. Nothing was off-limits.

Occasionally as we talked we would pull a sculpin or Irish Lord over the rail—spiky, large-headed, slender-bodied, worm-filled, bottom-dwelling fish that would roll when they hit the net, becoming woefully entangled by the time they came aboard. I would carefully extract them, unwinding web from about their prickly bodies, while trying to avoid the ghastly spears that jutted from their heads. These could penetrate the toughest glove and would actually inject bacteria and inflict something commonly called "fish poisoning." Bob, however, would unflinchingly smash them over the head, and pull them out the simplest way possible, before discarding their remains overboard. "They're just going to get stuck again," he'd say, the annoyance in his voice emphasizing his point each time, whether it was him or me pulling them from the net.

Finally, seeing my look of disapproval after knocking one dead against the rail of the boat and tossing its lifeless body back to the sea, he turned to me. "So, I suppose that means I'm not going to heaven," he challenged.

I looked back. "No," I replied after a silence, "what it means is you're probably coming back as one of them." A long moment passed between us, before we simultaneously burst into laughter. I noticed, from that time forward, that Bob began untangling the creatures, and while he might have at first made a joke of it, saying he was making amends, he did throw them back alive.

During this time we pulled one of the skiffs out of the water for repairs, and Bob was astounded when he noticed the large crack along its transom. I explained that it had likely occurred when Jackie so blatantly ignored my warnings about the rocks, just cruising along, not only cracking the bottom of the boat but also taking a bite out of the skeg of the motor when he hit. I relayed to Bob the smug satisfaction I had felt when it happened. After that, we began to put everything on Jackie. A hole in the net? Jackie must have done it. Anchors out of place? Jackie's fault. We even began to blame the rain and the mosquitoes on the poor guy.

As it turned out I had been right about Bob; he was a little like Woody in certain ways, and Mark, but also a lot like me. We shared an affinity for the outdoors, a reverence for the wilderness, and a love of all things outside the hand of man. It's where we found our solace. And while neither of us would have used the word God to describe it, we each felt a connection to something larger than ourselves out here. And on weekends, when fishing was closed, we'd seek it out, exploring the lonely beauty of places like Hidden Bay or the humbling grandeur of Chenega Glacier. Prince William Sound is home to any number of startling locales that because of their rugged landscape and distinct natural architecture defy everyday description and even lay beyond the grip of ordinary comprehension. This feeling of awe and gratitude is also something I found can just as easily reside in the simple—an afternoon spent swimming an alpine lake with the Linville kids, skipping rocks, examining water beetles—as well as in those moments of sheer amazement. There were so many of both, those moments of surprise that seem so much more common out here. Even instances that pierce the ambivalence of adolescence, witnessed through the eyes of the Linville children when an apparition, be it a humpback or an orca, suddenly appears out of the blue and breaches an arm's length from the boat.

I learned early on that the reason Bob setnetted, the reason he made it his job, was because it allowed him to live here in Prince William Sound for months on end. Without it, he explained, we would have simply been passing through, guests on vacation, not privy to the intimacies that living here can afford. Even the simple acts of daily life—gathering wood, building a fire, even doing the dishes—needed to be done in time with nature and took on an importance you wouldn't consider in town, allowing you a glimpse into something profound. It is the very job itself that has granted us acceptance into an ancient ritual, a drama tied inextricably to the change of tide, the phases of the moon, and the seemingly miraculous return of the fish. It is a quickly fading life of individualism and reciprocity, and one that fishermen have led for generations.

And Bob, with both the patience and reproof of an older brother, would begin to fill me in on all the secrets of fishing. He would take a neophyte with no obvious affinity for this type of work and mold him into not only a capable and confident hand, but a capable and confident man, demanding—often in a rather gruff fashion—a certain level of competence. He expected a job to get done to certain specifications, while at the same time allowing the space to get there on my own.

One of my initial tests came as we neared the end of that inaugural setnet season. Bob had left me alone with only a chain hoist and a few pieces of sage advice. He wanted the larger of our two skiffs hauled above tide-line and into the woods to be flipped for winter. It was a daunting task that at first appeared completely beyond the realm of possibility. As I slowly cranked with a come-along and chain hoist and watched the skiff move first up the beach and later onto its side and then over—a feat engineered through my own wits and just a bit of muscle—I found myself filled with an astonishing sense of satisfaction. It was a task that held in its completion an untold payoff in the form of accomplishment and self-worth. This was the first of many such impossible tasks around camp that accumulated into experience over the years, and without me realizing it, they settled into the flux of my everyday life until I finally reached a comfort level never dreamed of in those first tenuous weeks.

Over the seasons that followed, I would at least have a say in who our other deckhands might be and help train them, showing those who signed up how to fine-tune the anchors, set just so, a tangle of lines strewn between them and holding them in place, spun like some impossible web over the water. I would describe to them how to use the tide to our advantage when setting the gear, and calm them when the outboard would scream in reverse during our first openers, water splashing over the transom, the net spilling over the bow in a bizarre dance of hooks and lines. It was almost as if I were in charge—at least at the beginning of the season—even in those years when Patty and I would do most of the fishing. However, about halfway through the season, when fishing would pick up and Bob would trade the drift boat for the setnet site, I would have to figure out how to adjust. No longer would I tinker with the gear, decide when to wash it, or choose when to take a break. These were decisions that were made by consensus even when fishing with Patty. Now, with Bob's return, all decisions would suddenly be made by decree. I would be at once forced to deviate from my schedule, from "my-time" to "Bob-time." For many deckhands this would be an impossible proposition, often a deal breaker. But my ability to go with it, to be on "Bob-time," was what made me a good fit and why I stayed when others left. And Bob knew it. It's why he paid me a high percentage and often an extra bonus to keep me coming back. But I would have come back anyway. He doesn't know it, but he played a large part in who I have become. He is why I can now work on various boats without fear or worry and why, with complete confidence, I can even run a boat and a crew.

And as I watched the kids grow over the years into wide-eyed teenagers, I felt at least a part of their growth, a small part of the family. It's that way when you are living together, and in such close quarters. I'd even had my own father visit, my real family invited and welcomed for the better part of the season by my surrogate one. My father earned his keep as nanny and cook and by the end of the year might have hung his shingle out as master net-mender. But what really made an indelible impression was not the meals he cooked or the nets he hung, nor was it the special times we spent sport fishing or walking the beaches. No, it was simply seeing him here within this vast circle of life, a cycle logged not in years or days, but in ages and phases as slow as the wearing away of shoreline by sea. As ephemeral, as fleeting, as the passing of clouds, something which made his presence all the more profound, having

him on the beach, a part of three generations. Seeing the children, remembering what it was like to be in their place, I recalled how secure I had felt when this man was my age—I had been sure he knew everything because he carried himself that way, the same way Bob, the other fishermen, and I do now. I knew too, because of this cycle and our place in it, that before long I would stand in my father's stead once again, respected for my years but doted on by the youngsters who are suddenly so full of themselves. Funny, but of all the things that might have come to mind, it was this image— this moment—that struck me later on the *Iliamna Bay* when the shit hit the fan.

32

THE EDGE OF THE ABYSS

ILIAMNA BAY, APRIL 1997

"**I** DON'T THINK THERE'S any skipper that wants to go there," Tim said as we set a course toward Cape Pearce and the edge of the Bering Sea. It was still early afternoon and we had about an hour run out to where we would fish in a strait formed by a large island and a distinct point of land, ranging from eight to twelve miles across. Here, a series of narrow bays dotted the northwest shore, one of which held our quarry. "We might not even make it out there by the time they call the opener," said Tim, almost sounding like he was hoping that would be the case. He knew what he was doing, though; by now I had complete confidence in him and this boat and its crew. And despite the fog and low ceiling, the waters remained calm.

As is usual at the outset of an opening, a bit of hysteria ensued. Before setting out, we'd frantically tried to locate our pilot in order to refuel him. When we found him, Tim once again attempted unsuccessfully to persuade him to stay put. But both men knew there was little hope of us re-locating the large ball of herring without his eyes in the sky. He'd at least take off and attempt to pick his way through the clouds as we set course and once again pushed the engines of the *Iliamna Bay* in a race to reach the fish before an opening was called.

When we arrived on scene, it was already mid-afternoon and what we found was odd. With only two other boats in sight—and

then a long way off—it was a far cry from the war scene that usually raged on the herring grounds. We figured the other boats' pilots had likely risked an earlier flight, but there was no sign of them now. Only one plane—ours—passed low between the falling cover and the eerily calm seas.

In the flat light and haze it was difficult to find the fish. At the pilot's suggestion, Tim climbed into the crow's nest and steered the boat from there. He circled the boat, following the pilot's instructions until he finally spotted the school. When he did, he marveled at its dimensions; the school, maybe millions of fish, turning the water black along a sandy beach at the far head of one of the small bays. "All in all, a pretty good place to set," he shouted down to us. That was, of course, if they stayed put.

We all wondered what Fish and Game was waiting for—maybe they were deciding at the last minute whether to even have an opening at all. Maybe the roe wasn't quite ripe or perhaps the weather was too bad and they wanted more planes in the air. On the other hand, maybe they were glad there weren't more planes flying, so the catch would be limited.

In the meantime, the two other boats, knowing our pilot was the one in the air, had changed course and were beginning to head our way. That's when Tim took immediate, evasive action, turning off the fish in the hopes of luring the other vessels away. His deception worked—the other boats began to veer off. But the fish also began to move. They were now streaming down the beach and out of range. Then, as it does with herring, everything happened at once. The Department announced the opening was on and soon thereafter, the countdown began: 5-4-3-2-1. We had just twenty minutes, but the fish were no longer anywhere nearby. Where in the hell had they gone? We could also no longer hear our plane; the pilot likely thought we were on the herring and had headed to safer skies. Five minutes had passed by and we still hadn't spotted our herring. Perhaps they were moving faster down that beach than we thought—maybe even out into the open. That's when the sound of a lone engine, lost in the soup somewhere above, pierced the breathless air. Tim had obviously relayed our situation to the pilot, that we had lost the fish, yet at the same time assuring him that we would find them and that he should leave us to it. But now ten minutes had gone by and we still hadn't spotted them. Then we all watched in wonder as our plane—in what Tim would later refer to as the most courageous and talented move he'd ever witnessed—angled down out of the clouds through a sudden hole. With barely a wingspan of sky and wisps of sunshine behind him, he appeared as if through a small door, allowing him just enough leeway to sweep in before it closed. Down the beach he sailed in search of our lost fish, finally dropping a wing and pointing out exactly where they had gone.

Moving much faster than we'd ever anticipated, the herring were still fleeing en masse, veering along the mainland, and at each interval hiding themselves in a continually worse spot. Tim made a quick calculation and throttled ahead, taking a bead on the fish like a linebacker heading off an escaping ball carrier, deciding in this case where to lay our gear. Unfortunately, in this game there was no referee to blow the whistle, to call them out of bounds, and we went ahead and made our set, now just outside the slight protection the little bay afforded and within view of the outstretched finger of land separating us from the open sea.

33

SOMETIMES CATCHING THEM, THAT'S THE EASY PART

UNLIKE SALMON SEINING, where time is usually in large supply and the crews often work by rote, no two herring sets are ever the same, nor has an opener ever gone off like clockwork. Each one borders on the slightly insane, even when there are no other vessels to fend off. Due to the lack of time, an unfamiliar location, or the position of the boat, lashed off quickly to the tender and the net in a myriad of odd ways—it is extremely dangerous, even under the best of conditions. Then, if you are lucky and have a good catch, there's enough fish tied off between you and the tender to potentially sink your vessels. All of it compounds the strain both on the equipment and on your psyche, on the gear and rigging and your nerves. And as we adroitly closed this set off, we knew it was big. Tim estimated it was at least two hundred tons, maybe as many as three hundred or four hundred, and at three hundred dollars a ton it was a major payday; this made the whole process that much more tense and intense.

The lone tender that had followed us pulled along the outside of our gear, between us and the mainland, as we hurriedly pursed the seine, pulling the lead line up under the fish and sealing them in a bag of net beneath us. The tender crew quickly tied the cork line to their boat any way they could, in the usual slap-dash fashion, using the slight sway of the ocean to lay the line—burdened by the weight of thousands upon thousands of these small fish—onto a series of hooks attached to a thick steel cable festooned for just this purpose along the side of their vessel. Once it was fastened, a company representative tested the fish for ripeness; the higher the percentage of ripe roe, the higher the price we would be paid. It looked good, very good, and as they began to suction the herring aboard, filling their hold, we began to relax and to feel the throes of celebration set in. We were all going to be rich—at least several thousands of dollars richer!

Over the next several hours the fish were tested and pumped, and evening began to settle in. By the time the eighty-five-ton capacity of our tender was reached, it was turning toward dusk. Another tender, which would tie up along the outside of this one and "pump across," was at least three or four hours away, and a third, which we'd surely need for such a large haul would certainly be sent by the company, and hopefully just behind it. With our tender anchored and holding us in place, we'd wait. It was calm. The sky actually looked like it was beginning to clear a little.

Butch, the skipper of the *Sea Mist*, likely had far more experience herring fishing than just about anyone in our group, and from the beginning he had expressed qualms about even heading out to where the set had been made. He knew, however, that he had a duty to his partners to be there now to help out and to make sure all went well with us. He and his crewmen, including Greg, had watched as the net was sealed, the set finished, and the tender began to pump fish aboard.

"In my mind it was in the bag," Greg said later, but Butch hadn't been so sure.

"We're not going to go far," Butch insisted, even after our first 85 tons were pumped and his crew, after enduring what seemed an interminable period of standing by, had long grown bored. "I've been in these deals before. Sometimes catching the fish, that's the easy part. They're not ours until they're on the tender.

Actually," he said, amending his initial statement, "they're not ours until we've been paid for them."

It was something Greg would always remember. He'd been fishing long enough to know Butch was right. Still, waiting is never easy even though fishermen are used to it, and Butch could see his crew was antsy. He was too. After all the build-up, all the running around, they hadn't even made a set themselves and some of that energy remained. After several restless hours, he sent Greg and his skiff man over to see if there was something for them to do, anything to get them off the boat for a while. "Might as well go over there and help babysit the set," he said. "You never know."

On the *Iliamna Bay*, we were in celebration mode. After all, our work was done. The other tenders would arrive, finish pumping our fish out, we'd do a little clean-up and go to bed, and tomorrow we'd wake up much wealthier than when we started the day. But we waited and kept waiting. We ate dinner, we had a beer, and Karl even suggested it might be time to break out the whiskey. I initially thought why not? If nothing else it would be a good way to pass the time. I was a little surprised when Brad declined. "Let's wait until we're really done," he said and I agreed. Karl too. It was getting late and we all wanted it to be over with, to be unloaded and on our way. So instead we played a game of cards. I even laid down for an hour, but I couldn't sleep. It had grown dark as we marked our time, continually wondering where in the hell those tenders were.

"Still on their way," said Tim each time we'd ask. He'd been on the radio with them at least a dozen times. The company obviously hadn't thought we'd set so far out or hadn't planned on us catching so many fish. Besides, these big boats are slow, some only traveling seven or eight knots an hour, which might mean as many as four or five hours of travel time to where we were. And I'd worked for these companies before—who knew how long it had taken them to decide which boat to send. They may even have had the boats run an errand first.

I went to the deck and scanned the horizon. It was pitch black by now, and I could only see a couple small twinkles, boat lights like stars lost in the distance, so far off they might as well have been in another galaxy. That's when I heard the skiff. It seemed to almost pop out of nowhere and into the bright glow of our halogen lights, which swept in a semi-circle just out beyond our deck. These giant lights lit up the *Iliamna Bay* like a stadium, but also left you wondering what was happening just beyond them, on the periphery, where everything just dissolved into the darkness. The skiff entered from behind a black curtain, appearing as if by magic at the side of our boat.

"Butch sent us over to see if there's anything we can do," announced Greg as he climbed over the rail. We welcomed him aboard but told him there really wasn't much.

Still we were glad to see a couple new faces, hear a new story, anything to break up the monotony. Brad was on his way across to the tender to take a shower. "Might as well not let that boat and all their water go to waste," he said before climbing to our bow. We were tied off, our bow to the tender's stern, by a line that had grown exceedingly tight. Brad had to take a step or two across it like a tightrope walker to get to the other boat. I watched him suspended a few feet above the ocean, then noticed that the water below us was no longer placid and had begun to stir. It was running like a river between the two vessels now, signifying a tide change. We'd been through at least one since we'd set, so I didn't think too much of it at the moment. But the tide had just started shifting and I really hadn't paid too much attention to the clock either, other than logging off the hours waiting for an additional tender, so I didn't know it was just beginning to roar. If I had only made the connection, that the tide had just started and was already running so hard, I might have known what was brewing and relayed it to the others.

Back on deck we still hadn't noticed much of a change in the ocean. Karl offered our guests something to drink as we hashed over the usual topics—the price of fish and how ready we were to head home. But before long, we couldn't help but notice it. It came first on the *Iliamna Bay*. The two boats tied together were facing opposite directions, the back of ours aligned with the bow of the tender, which was anchored into the short, oncoming waves. With our stern into the waves we took the brunt of them as they abruptly built into a froth, at first just rocking the *Iliamna Bay*. And then, seemingly without warning—though in reality these churning seas may have been intensifying for as much as an hour—they erupted, now rocking even the larger boat, the one facing into them. Our initial thought, after having sat stationary, with nary a breath of wind for so long, was "what the fuck is going on?" I saw the tender's skipper peer out of the door on his bridge a story above us, his face creased with a look of bewilderment and concern. The way he hurried back and forth didn't rest well with me. We all thought the weather had taken an immediate and drastic turn. Oddly, there was still none of the wind that would accompany a squall, but no one seemed to notice in the increasing frenzy. We were trapped in our little sphere of light, like one of those globes that hold a winter scene, only we were held tightly to the now roiling whitecaps, building in force, beginning to wash over our stern. Our situation, having all at once gone from one of celebration to one of dread, had taken a precipitous about-face.

34

CUTTING LOSSES

ON THE *RAFFERTY*, Grant awoke with a start out of a sound sleep. The rest of his crew, as well as our pilot, had turned in soon after anchoring and safely hoisting the small plane on deck. But now he found himself suddenly jolted awake. "I've always had a sixth sense about these things," he later said, "and I had a really awful, almost sick feeling."

He also thought he might have heard voices on the radio, but the only one he might have picked up from our group was Tim, talking to the tender that was supposedly on its way. Tim likely had more urgency in his voice. Whether it was the radio or just his premonition, Grant was awake now and sure something had gone terribly wrong.

He had anchored the *Rafferty* nearby just in case, and after waking he left a note for his crew, letting them know he had taken their skiff into the darkness and headed our way.

When he arrived, the tide rip running between the island and mainland and between the two boats had intensified, and with it every line—at least a dozen of them, tied helter-skelter to the gear and between the vessels—had grown as tight as piano wires. The tide was running so fast that Grant was forced to fully throttle the skiff just to hold it in place long enough for someone to tie it off. Tim seemed glad to see the other skipper, to have someone onboard who had seen his share of these situations and with whom he might confer. They agreed that things were still holding together, there was still hope of saving the set.

"The first thing we need to do is something about that," said Grant, pointing up towards the rigging.

The net, suspended from the boom and hanging down through the block, had so much force upon it created by the bag of now-dead fish—perhaps as much as two hundred tons or more of dead weight just hanging between us and being pulled by the current—that the fittings had begun to leak. Long before, a line had been tied from the corks, where they rose off the boat to a deck cleat in an attempt to alleviate some of the strain on the fittings and hopefully prolong—at least for the immediate future—the life of the equipment. Despite being a line so thick you'd have tied an enormous ship up with it, it appeared to be at about its limit.

At that moment it became obvious to me why Grant had experienced so many Oh Shit Moments. He'd rather do something dangerous himself than ask someone else to do it. So, armed with a pocketful of tools, he began to climb the mast and then shimmy out onto the boom so he could tighten the fittings. We watched as he called down to tell us how precarious his makeshift seat was; it was shuddering with all that pressure on it. All I could do was shake my head. If something were to give at that moment he'd be in the worst kind of trouble. I was glad it was someone else's call, glad I wasn't in his place or making the decision to send someone up there. It seemed like an eternity, but he made it down. "I'm not sure how long that's going to hold," he said as he reached the deck.

It wasn't just the seas that had changed over the previous couple of hours. Everyone on board had grown accordingly anxious, until it felt as if the situation was finally on the verge of being beyond our control. Not a situation you ever want to encounter aboard a boat.

For each of us it began at a different interval, that sudden stark realization that things weren't right, and later that they had actually hit the fan. Sometime long before Grant had even come aboard,

Brad—still in the shower—had felt the tender swaying and heard the muffled calls of the crew echoing through its cavernous hallways. He dressed quickly, anxious to discover what was going on. Everything had been quiet to the point of tedium when he left the *Iliamna Bay.*

More than once as the seas worsened, I found myself, along with Greg or Karl or the crew aboard the tender, suggesting it was time to get out from under these fish and cut our losses. We huddled on deck at various times discussing when and how we might do just that. Tim, Grant, and occasionally Greg would jump in. I could read in the faces of these men—men who had made their lives at sea—an uncustomary disquietude, plagued by a deep and rapidly growing concern as their talk shifted from saving the fish to saving the boat. Despite their dismay, they continued calmly discussing how we might get out of this jam and fish another day.

I was still confident we'd figure this out. *These guys know what they're doing*, I thought. *We'll get it.* That's when the tenderman emerged, wild-eyed and screaming from his wheelhouse, shouting something about running aground. Peering down from the metal balcony that surrounded the cabin, he at first appeared to be shouting at no one in particular, to the elements, before his rabid gaze took a laser-like turn and honed in on Tim. Instantly I felt it, the first pangs of disbelief and true anguish rising from the very depths of my bowels. Seeing this man who only hours ago appeared so confident and sure of himself suddenly in a panic was unnerving to say the least—not to mention being informed in such a harrowed cry that the anchor had finally given up its hold and that we were slowly being dragged toward our demise on the rocky mainland.

Tim immediately attempted to calm him. Despite the crisis, the adrenaline that must have been feeding his own alarm, Tim managed to maintain his control and spoke in a subdued tone, assuring the tenderman and all of us that things would be okay. "Don't worry," he said repeatedly, "we are going to figure this out."

He would send both skiffs, ours and the *Sea Mist*'s, off to begin pulling on the vessels and the set to keep it and us from running aground. In no time Karl and the other skiffman had donned Mustang suits and we were loading towlines and preparing the skiffs for their mission. We were happy for the briefest respite, a moment to have something to occupy our minds and to try in any way to manage our fates.

At various junctures over the intervening hours or minutes—which seemed to coalesce, to collide and infuse, at once unending, vaporous and obscured by the course of events—there were many strange pauses. At some point during one of these, maybe almost subconsciously or as a mere passing thought, Tim noticed that as we dragged, as the ball of dead fish and the boats floated as one, the pressure was momentarily released on our equipment, water ceased crashing over our stern, and the *Iliamna Bay*, although it was moving, felt almost stationary.

This is when, during one of the tenderman's frequent appearances outside his wheelhouse, the conversation became decidedly heated. Tim implored him more forcefully each time he emerged to please lift his anchor, so that we would move in unison, the exact opposite of what he wanted to do. The tenderman was beside himself, insisting that despite the skiffs' efforts at holding us at bay, we would be sucked into the point of land and torn to pieces on its jagged shores. I didn't know what to think. Regardless of his state, it seemed to me he might be right.

"No," insisted Tim, "the skiffs will hold us off and the current carry us free." I remember thinking how frantic the conversation had become, shouted between decks, and I couldn't believe how long it went on. The tenderman continually disappeared inside only to emerge again, agitated and wild, asking what in the hell we were going to do, and refusing to take Tim's suggestion.

Between these episodes, we'd been attempting to decide which lines needed to be cut in order to release our once enviable and now perilous load. We let the pucker line go—the purse of the seine—but the long-dead fish went nowhere. With the seas running continually harder, each time the anchor caught, their massive weight continued with the tide to test our gear to its limits. Now violently rocking the boat, the seas washed over our stern with a renewed vigor, threatening anything on deck that was not lashed down—including our crew. Tim somehow remained calm and methodical as he attempted to decide which line to cut, hoping for the one that would all at once allow our escape from these ill-fated fish. He knew cutting the wrong one could send the boat heeling completely over. On his order, I pulled the small serrated knife taped to my shoulder from its sheath; knives we all carry on our raingear in case of emergency, in case we get wound up in gear like in my old nightmare. No force, no sawing motion required. Barely did I touch the inch-thick line that strained from a pulley on our small starboard boom and it separated in a loud burst. Released all at once, the boom bounced overhead with a sudden vehemence that sent a shockwave through everyone within its vicinity and sent us ducking for cover. But as we returned to our feet we saw that the fish remained. Now that we had them we couldn't seem to let them go.

By this time, the skiffs had been pulling for hours. I would catch a glimpse of them from time to time on the periphery of our deck lights, side by side. Karl and the other driver called back and forth between their boats, smiling, laughing even. *What in the hell are they so happy about?* I thought to myself. Later I'd find out that all the time they'd been out in the darkness, motors revving, they'd thought they were holding us in place, oblivious to the drama playing out just a hundred feet away.

Finally, at some point the tenderman, looking for an answer, willing to do just about anything, finally gave in and ordered his crew to pull anchor. On deck, we knew we had a temporary reprieve. However, there wasn't one of us, including Tim, who didn't entertain at least the possibility of running aground—the unthinkable lingering in the back of our minds. Yet we knew this had bought us a little leeway, the incredible force on our gear letting up slightly and giving us a precious block of time to decipher which lines to cut, which lines would free us from these blasted fish.

Grant, later followed by Greg, had decided to board the tender in order to try and gain a sense of where we were and how we were moving. On the bridge, still shrouded in darkness, Grant examined the radar, looking at it again and again. He couldn't believe how far we'd moved over the course of the night, as many as fifteen or even twenty miles. It didn't seem possible. By his calculations we were still at least half a mile off shore, nearly beyond the little point of land, and in at least sixty feet of water.

It looked like Tim's initial feeling had been correct; if we'd continued to drift we'd have likely moved into the open ocean. It dawned on Grant then that this was some sort of immense, anomalous tide rip and not a weather problem. *There's no wind*, he thought to himself, *we'll be in the clear soon*. We were beyond saving the set, but at least we'd save the boat. But the tenderman would have none of it, still insisting, on the verge of complete hysteria, that we would run aground. Our end was near, our boats about to be shattered to pieces.

"Come here," pleaded Grant, both he and Greg insisting the tenderman look closely at his radar. "We did everything but try and restrain him physically," they would say later. But sure he was going to lose his boat, he gave the order to drop the anchor once again. And that was it.

35

HITTING THE FAN

As THE SEAS and the situation continued to intensify, time had become more obscure, almost meaningless—lost. There was a point, Greg said later, where everything seemed to be out of control, everyone running around doing their own thing, slightly panicked and crazy. Tim said he finally had to put what the tenderman was doing out of his mind, that he was tired of arguing with him. But he couldn't believe it—none of us could—when the anchor dropped again. It bounced slightly before digging in. Suddenly the pressure on the rigging above our heads and straining at the net between the two boats increased at least tenfold, the stern now completely awash in seawater. With the two boats stopped so short and with such force, the bow of the tender actually started dipping to the current line, and with it I could tell I wasn't the only one who had gone from guarded and concerned to scared.

The tenderman was now sure his boat was going to be pulled under. Nothing could hold up to this, something was going to give and give right away. And it wasn't going to be pretty.

There was no doubt the anchor was now intractably set, and with us attached there was no way for the tender to power into the current, above it and pull it. There was absolutely nothing anyone could do to make it come loose, and with its inextricable hold the situation had lost all sense of proportion and reason. Emotions were running high and suddenly it was no holds barred.

Tim, from our boat, and Grant, still aboard the tender, were now visibly shaken, crying out that the anchor line must be cut and cut now, or we were going to lose one or maybe both boats, or even worse. It was a refrain echoed across the decks for what seemed an eternity. Yet when the crew of the tender appeared on deck with a grinder, rather than our anchor line they started cutting at the cable holding our cork line, the only thing really keeping the two boats solidly linked together. Apparently the tenderman had decided to hell with us—it was time to be done with this and cut his boat free.

At first I conveniently blocked the incident from my mind. Even years later, recounting the scenes for someone they play back with a dreamlike, illusory quality, my muscles contracting, the small hairs on the back of my neck rising to the attention of a cold chill. It's almost as if seeing it from elsewhere, watching it from afar . . .

Time, still meaningless, has accelerated and in the blink of an eye turned completely mad. Greg is right, all independence has been lost, seized by an outside force. We are no longer in control of the situation, it now controls us. There is no more quiet pondering, trying to decipher which line to cut. We will quickly cut all remaining lines one by one in the hopes that the fish and net might go before the boat does, its stern now perpetually covered in water, the waves outpacing it, washing over it before the stern can completely drain. And time, meaningless time, however much we have left, is running out and running out fast.

We cut one line, gingerly stepping forward, reaching out as we turn slightly sideways, shielding ourselves from its reverberation, a release of energy that we know is coming. But perhaps knowing it's coming makes it worse. Each laceration of a line and its successive blast sends us stumbling backwards in its aftermath. First one and then another. But to no avail. The fish remain—until the third or fourth line, that is. Then it's as if we have unleashed a demon. To a man, we step back in witness to the raw power and efficiency with which the net is being propelled from our deck, with a vehe-

mence and a velocity one would never have imagined possible. All at once the entire net spools up and over the block and out between the two boats, toward our bow and the open ocean. There's no way to stop it, to slow its departure. The only time I can remember feeling this helpless—subject to the whim of forces beyond my control—was during an earthquake. Don't even go near it, Tim shouts, as a couple of us try to aid its departure, to make sure it doesn't backlash. If the net gets caught up on itself it will likely stall and rip the boat to pieces, it's going that fast. Stay back, stay back, Tim shouts as he hits the hydraulics in an effort to speed up the block, which is on the verge of burning out, the seine rising off the deck and out in a tumult. This must be taking longer than I think, because Tim even has time to rev the engine in an effort to compensate, to speed the big pulley up even further. It seems to be keeping up, for now.

Then suddenly the corks, in a rapid staccato, begin to skip over the davit. A series of small rollers on the end of a heavy steel bar, it is attached along the rail of the boat with a large pin so that it can be removed and placed on either side of the vessel—a device integral to seining but one that we usually barely give a second thought to. As the corks ricochet off its head, I tell myself this can't get any worse, but its obvious to all aboard it's about to. In an instant they catch, corks clamping tight between the davit and the rail. It occurs so fast none of us can quite fathom what is suddenly happening.

Oh shit, someone yells. Our boat, this forty-two-foot vessel, our home that has endured the worst seas, suddenly heaves thirty or forty degrees starboard, as if it is weightless, as if it is made of balsa wood. Our rigging must be just about hitting the tender. Water washes over the rail, against my knees, crashing against the cabin. I steady myself. With all we've been through I've never actually pictured it, but now I'm sure: we are going down. I push on the corks—it's the only thing left to do. Certainly they are too heavy to unseat by myself but perhaps it's adrenaline or more likely the sway of the ocean, but they dislodge. The Iliamna Bay *rights itself, but only partially and momentarily, just enough for the dreaded beat of the corks to resume. It's a strangely timed syncopation that signals our end. Just a few shallow breaths and they catch, once again lurching us over to port. Each time I'm sure we are done for and push for all I'm worth. Brad is standing next to me. Tim screams for the two of us to be careful, then in a fevered pitch gives the order for Brad to pull the pin on the davit. But I'm too close, and the net is never very far off. All at once, just like my dream, I'm ensnared. Entwined in net and off my feet. Though it's happening so fast, I know what's going on, see it all, as if from above as well as from within. Flying through the air. My right arm and shoulder, my torso, my head are entangled, the net like a twisted cocoon wrapped around me as I leave my feet. There's no escape. No way to pull my knife, no time to cut. I'm finished, a goner, I know it. My left shoulder slams against the cabin. I'm still here. I reach out, holding on for all that is dear. Instinctively pulling, flailing, fighting with every fiber of my being, grasping at survival.*

Tim says he grabbed me. Brad initially said no, it was him. But Grant doesn't remember it like that at all. It happened too fast for anyone to stop me. I was gone in an instant, completely out of sight around the cabin, he said later. He was sure when I appeared back on deck that I'd at least be missing an arm or a leg.

If someone did grab me, I'm eternally grateful. What I do know is that my head was so ensnarled I lost my glasses. One shoulder was wrenched in the net and the other slammed into the side of the boat, but neither was sore until days later—shock superseding even the slightest notion of pain. Somehow, whether my shipmates pulled me to safety or I caught the cabin just right to free myself, I fell back in a heap on deck and somehow, as Tim would say later, miraculously intact, at least physically.

I feel someone lift me to my feet and I'm suddenly surrounded. Even with all that is going on there's a pause, faces in rapt attention asking if I am all right. *Are you sure?* asks Tim, his hands on my shoulders, his eyes wide and barely inches from mine. *Oh my God, I can't believe you're okay!* exclaims Brad, stammering, almost shouting in my ear. *He's as visibly shaken as I am, but his excitement, his adrenaline, the loudness of his voice are in direct opposition to my stunned silence. Oh my God, dude; God, I can't believe you're alive, he continues. But there's no time. The net is still plummeting downward, it and everyone around me out of control. One of the tender's crewmen is still frantically grinding away on the cable, for what now has seemed an eternity. Time continues to pass at strange intervals. I'm not sure what's happening, can't see very well without my glasses, my knees shake involuntarily. I can't seem to stop them. It's not so much fear but confusion, a vast blanket of confusion and disorder. Death is no longer an obscure and random thought and it continues to be present. I've escaped it, barely, but I know only for the time being. It remains here on deck like an apparition, or perhaps like a stowaway that's always been here, reminding me I'm still alive. Even through the confusion one thought persists—I shouldn't be. Holy shit, I mutter aloud, I can't believe it, over and over again.*

I hardly notice but Grant, sure it's the end, has gotten off the boat and into his skiff. He's untied it, so it won't be pulled down by the Iliamna Bay *when she finally goes. Cut loose, it's an island, he says, our only safety valve, and he's getting ready to rescue those of us who survive. Once again his intuition is right. In what can only be a matter of minutes, the grinder finally eats through that cable with its long line of hooks, the only thing—other than the block—left holding our net, which is quickly nearing its end. But we are still attached, the net continuing to plunge violently into the sea. I haven't really put it together, but when that cable goes, the net's sudden departure from the tender is like a catapult, the final ultimate sum of energy released, and what we feared most. It's built up to this point, there's no answer, nothing that can stand in its way. The ball of fish shackled between our boats is going with the current and there's no stopping it, its departure savage and final. Oh shit, is all I have time to say to myself. Here we go again, I think. How can this be?*

In an instant the boom, as if it were just a twig, snaps in half. It plows like a battering ram through our rigging, smashing deck lights and sending a stream of sparks skyward, to explode like deadly fireworks overhead. Hydraulic lines burst, an unctuous rain coats the deck in a hot, slippery, and flammable film. I feel Tim grabbing me and then Brad, simultaneously pulling us underneath the overhanging lip of the cabin. Karl and the other skiffman, who must have come aboard at some point, scurry for Grant's skiff. How easily they, or any one of us, might have been crushed by the falling block, which has splintered the fiberglass bin boards covering our hold and left fabricated steel along the rail hopelessly scarred.

Off, Tim shouts, now. I feel his hands on my back leading me, pulling, pushing me. We are going down. Even Tim is sure of it. I need to reach the skiff before that happens, before I'm nearly cast into the ocean again. It's a scramble into Grant's boat, his island, the second time I've escaped with my life.

Karl and the other skiffman are already there, joining Brad, Tim, and me. Only Greg remains. With the boat listing far to starboard, he scuttles along the port rail as if on an off-kilter balance beam, precariously perched above the still-confused seas. No one's asked him to do it, but he knows, intuitively, from years at sea that as a last act he must sever the remaining lines binding the two boats together, before jumping aboard the skiff.

This is it. The possibility you're always aware of, but for all the close calls, near misses, and Oh Shit Moments, most guys go their whole careers without having to abandon ship. If you thought it would really happen, why even go? But it's happening now, and Greg, from the minute he jumps aboard, says he can feel Tim's bulking frame involuntarily shaking, seeing his boat, knowing it's going down. But Tim is also the first to give thanks.

Thank God we're all alive, he says, almost in supplication, thank God everyone is okay. Far worse than losing the boat would have been losing one of his crewmen.

All we can do is move along with the boat, just watching and feeling the ocean. Then, just as suddenly as it all started, it stops. It's as if someone has literally turned off a switch. The ocean, in all its fickle glory and anger, has in an instant subsided, gone from vehement and bitter to shockingly, eerily still. Just as the day had begun, all at once we are in a flat, almost serene—though certainly surreal—calm. I notice then a distinct line, the blanket of thinning clouds ending and the sky in the distance aglow, the gathering light a lost virtue beginning to fill the air. At last we are emerging from darkness, which also means that we've been awake and at this for nearly twenty-four hours. And here we are. The Iliamna Bay, *as well as all of us, has somehow survived, miraculously—it's a word being thrown around a lot, even by the nonbelievers. The* Iliamna Bay *remains afloat, though as we pull up in silence, it's obvious she has not fared well. Abandoned to the unbridled power of the ocean, torn to pieces, shards of broken glass and rigging strewn across her normally neat and orderly deck, she appears like a ghost ship against the pale dawn. Only a battery-powered auxiliary lamp inside the cabin illuminates the carnage. I feel Tim's hand on my shoulder, feel it squeezing once and then twice, as he surveys the damage and mulls over what has happened. Then, in the distance, just beyond the thin mantle of clouds, a lone star, a comet, streaks across the horizon and dissolves into the atmosphere. Of all things, I think of my father on the beach at Main Bay, at the Linville's camp. I also recall the ill-begotten feeling inspired by that abandoned boat that we motored by not long ago at False Pass. I can feel what was once intractable dismay and turbulence beginning to subside, though it's already being replaced by something more amorphous—an insidious, over-riding fatigue and disillusionment that I fear will be impossible to cast aside. I can feel it worming its way in.*

36

AFTERMATH

SLEEP, WHEN IT did come, came only erratically, interrupted by dreams and nightmares, intermingling with bizarre thoughts and a conglomeration of people I hadn't seen in years, those I may have thought I'd wronged and those I'd simply lost track of. What did it mean? We'd all turned inward and dour. Surviving something like this must inspire these mysterious thoughts.

And it had begun last night, when we didn't have much choice but to climb back aboard the boat and attempt to make it habitable. We spent hours trying to scrub the slippery liquid that had spewed all over the deck, knowing we'd be skating for days. Then largely in silence and as best we could we secured the broken mast. As thought became more lucid we rehashed bits and pieces of the night in our minds, but never completely—only what might have forestalled the inevitable. If only our pilot hadn't found that hole in the clouds, if only the fish had moved along the beach a little faster and out to sea, we'd have been spared all of this.

What doesn't kill you only makes you stronger? I think it was Karl who repeated that old adage at one point. Yet I felt anything but strong. We like to think of ourselves as the center of the universe, as important and invulnerable. But later on, as I lay there and tried without hope to grab a few morsels of uninterrupted sleep I began to consider my place. I felt only small, ineffectual, and weak. All the nerve I had at one time possessed—I knew it wasn't always good, that it can make you do dumb things—nevertheless, I was sure, at least a small modicum of it was still essential; without it you wouldn't take even the slightest risk. Sure, it had naturally waned, but as I'd gotten older confidence had made up for it, or better yet superseded it. But this, it had shaken both and I didn't know when or if I'd get either of them back.

With no hydraulics and thus no anchor, at midmorning we found ourselves once again tied to the tender. Little was said as we retreated almost immediately to our bunks. Yet no one else fared any better at sleep and by early afternoon we were all up, though hardly awake, more like punch-drunk fighters after a brawl, completely beaten down, barely coherent, and universally exhausted.

"Man, I'm glad to see you, glad you're alive," Tim uttered occasionally. I had an inkling he might have been blaming himself or at least rehashing what he might have done differently. But I think we all knew it was the darkness. "If only we could have seen the other side of that rip, we would have known how calm it was," he said. "I really thought it was rough everywhere."

"We all did," said Karl.

"If we'd only known," lamented Tim, for a second, even a third time. He was right. If we'd known it would have changed everyone's attitude, everyone's train of thought. If it had been light, if we hadn't been held prisoner by the darkness, the tenderman might have been okay cutting his anchor line or likely not even dropped it a second time. Maybe Tim would have had the skiffs pull in a different direction, or he might have been able to put the boat in gear to keep up with the tide. Who knows? It's all too easy in hindsight. But he'd already begun directing his attention elsewhere, to what needed to be done to get home. He even thought we might fish again, though there seemed little hope of that and even less will on the part of our battered crew. We wanted no part of it. Brad had already told me that he just wanted out. And I couldn't seem to stop the haphazard thoughts coursing through my brain . . . my close escape, the sheer randomness of it all.

And so it was, with little fanfare and morale at near zero, we cut loose from the tender and headed to the processing barge, hoping that the floating factory with its little weld shop and street-smart engineers might help put us back together.

It may have been between shifts, but coffee, sweets, and sandwich fixings were always available. I should have been ravenous. My stomach wasn't full or tied in knots any longer, just not ready to accept food yet. Any change of scenery would have been welcome, but the sterility and the communal texture of the place felt offputting and strange. I was going on thirty-six hours now with little or no rest, at best hovering in that netherworld between wakefulness and sleep and still foggy. For some reason Tim had remained behind, tied off one hundred feet behind the processor. Maybe he was getting things prepared, or perhaps he had been brushed aside for the moment by the welders, who probably had their fill of projects and weren't too thrilled to see a wayward ship come calling for help. Either way, we were here, Karl and I. After our stop at the cafeteria we made our way down a series of long corridors that looked a lot like the cannery only more compressed. Still, the smells and the sounds of processing equipment—*Ka-chink, Ka-chink, Ka-chink*—echoing through the halls put me in mind of the old crew in Seward. I wished I was with them, in the campground, in the old fish plant, a place I never really liked but which now in memory actually seemed somehow safe and familiar. If only I wasn't so damn tired I would have left—jumped out of my skin and fled into the sea. But instead I followed Karl like a lost dog through the corridors, trying to find the showers. I wouldn't let him out of my sight; he was my only hold to something tangible, something known. Meanwhile, the steady beat of the processing equipment, like a mechanical heartbeat, grew continually louder and closer until we found ourselves standing in front of a glass door through which we could see the workers. All were wearing the same yellow raingear, standing in rows, preparing frozen herring to be shipped or stored. Only one of them was outside the door, still in his raingear, his brow damp with sweat despite the dank chill that always permeated the deep recesses of these boats, and his expression decidedly anguished.

"What's wrong?" asked Karl.

"Oh, the foreman caught me with chew," he said. He had obviously just spit it out and was catching a quick break.

"Well, don't feel bad," said Karl, turning his thumb toward me. "This guy here, he almost got killed last night."

The worker, as if taking notice of me for the first time, began his survey, our eyes meeting, a knowing look crossing his face. He smiled. It was a look of acknowledgment. He knew we weren't bullshitting. I smiled back, as sad and ironic as it was—my first since this whole episode had begun.

If time had become obscured during our ordeal, it now dragged to a standstill. Tim had focused all his attention and energy into fixing the boat—not only because it was something that needed to be done but likely as a way to avoid brooding over what had happened. As a result he spent the bulk of his time aboard the processor with its welders, who had probably realized he wasn't going anywhere until they had him running again. Someone had to remain on the *Iliamna Bay*, which bobbed behind the processing boat, dwarfed by its enormous blue hulk. Brad and I, likely too numb to see what was coming, remained silent. And I can't really blame Karl for speaking up. After all, he was out in the skiff through the worst of it; to him this entire event was probably little more than another Oh Shit Moment, and the last thing he wanted was to be left here in the cabin of the *Iliamna Bay* with his shell-shocked crewmates. So he was quick to volunteer. He'd go help Tim, leaving Brad and me to our own devices. We were little more than prisoners aboard our own boat, desperate prisoners in a cabin that was growing exceedingly smaller with each hour that passed.

Brad was first to say it, not just state it but decry it, his expression pained and eyes bloodshot, his voice distant and ranting. *I need to get out of here.* As soon as we were alone he began. "This whole thing is crazy. I need to get out of here now," he rambled, desperation rising like the tide, born of frustration and confinement, and that put me at once on edge and had me worried.

I tried my best to allay his fears. But how could I? Inside I felt exactly the same. "I don't want to be here either," I said in as commiserative a tone as I could muster. *We can't just leave, though. Where are we going to go? We have to fix the boat. What about Tim? We have to help him get the* Iliamna Bay *home.*

Thankfully I was able to keep my own, long percolating strife in check, and thankfully my feigned composure seemed to have an effect, not only on Brad but in convincing myself that I had a duty to stay. At some point during the next few days I could feel our mutual angst slowly subsiding into mere unrest, a featureless plodding void that only occasionally would flare into an outburst or panic. We tried our best, for each other's sake, to keep our mutual despair to a minimum, never allowing ourselves to erupt at the same time. One of us had to be able to subdue the other, to convince ourselves that we would survive and somehow eventually make it home.

It hardly mattered that we'd gotten the hydraulics back together and could anchor. We were still confined to our cell all day long. It probably didn't help that Brad and I were the ones who had read philosophy and had toyed with various religions. Of course in normal life it would have provided a welcome intellectual detour. But here, discussing God and our beliefs before jumping on to some other existentialist tangent, was not a good idea. Following the same blind road, only to finally reach the same sorry dead end, wondering whether there was any point to any of it, this was no consolation, and certainly no real diversion, not in this place, not now. No, here it was an added barrier to our well-being—at times perhaps to our very sanity—and a reason to turn repeatedly to our stashed whiskey. What the hell, at this point it didn't matter. I'd drink as much as I thought I could get away with.

For five days this went on. It was as if everything that occurred, everything we talked about, had some special meaning, a hidden agenda, and not necessarily one we could figure out. It didn't matter what it was. It could be a magazine article, maybe about clear-cutting the Amazonian rainforest or it might have been an epidemic in Africa, either way it must have had some hidden meaning, something to say concerning us and what had happened. Nothing was coincidence, and all we had was a desperate longing to make some sense of it, which also made it difficult to escape, to dissolve into a book or a movie, anything that might allow us to forget for a moment what we'd been through.

Of course there were brief interruptions, but they seemed no less portentous. One such event was when the *Sea Mist* came by to deliver our net. "Here it is," said Butch. All four of us—Karl and Tim on board at the time—listened with a chill to his story about the net's recovery. It happened when Greg and the skiff driver were still with us on the *Iliamna Bay*, so it was just Butch and his other crewman. Following the current, they'd found the unattached seine floating in that unearthly, pre-dawn light—a lone net by itself. With all that had happened, Butch said, it gave him a start at first to see the net out there with no boat nearby. But being the rational man he was he quickly pushed any portent aside and began the task at hand, made rather difficult with just the two of them. Once they'd wrestled the net over the block and began stacking it, things went smoothly enough. He had completely discarded any ill feelings and it was going along fine for five or ten minutes. But then, all at once, they were startled by the power block suddenly grinding to a halt. "It shocked me," said Butch, "I didn't know what had happened. It took a minute to realize we'd pulled something aboard, something heavy. When we reversed the block and lowered it we found this," he said, pointing. "It was tangled," he went on, "tangled bad in the gear." He pulled a tarp away and there it was—the davit. And what was it he had said, tangled, tangled bad? It could have been me with it. . . . We all stood still for a minute, just staring at it, at this cold, inanimate piece of steel.

"Well, there it is," I said. A bead of moisture and a shiver trickled down my spine.

"Nearly your downfall," added Karl.

I wasn't sure how to feel. I don't think anyone was. There was a nervous chuckle or two, but no one said anything and it seemed up to me to break the silence. "Well," I said, "we better get it back on board."

And so, without saying a word we passed it, almost ceremoniously, from one boat to the other.

There was a faint trace of relief, a catharsis in hauling it aboard. But there were other incidents that did nothing but intensify our longing to put a quick and merciful end to this incarceration. It happened just a few days later. Brad and I had finally begun to loosen up. We began planning a trip, sport fishing in an altogether different place, maybe even this summer, on a peaceful stream somewhere— a freshwater paradise far from the sea. It was likely our first real departure, something totally unrelated to what had occurred, but as we talked we heard a commotion on a vessel anchored only a few boats away. We knew right away something terrible had happened. We both felt it—that instantaneous sense of dismay that we had lived with since that night.

It would be hours until Tim solemnly delivered the news that one of their crewmen had been killed, crushed by skiff that fell as it was being hoisted over him. Though we were sure something was coming, it was as if a shiv had been twisted between my ribs. I looked at Brad and for just an instant spied that look of possession and helplessness, the one I'd seen on the first day of our jail sentence, our confinement to the boat. Then, just as quickly, I saw him swallow it down. He would attempt to fend it off, much like I had, saving it up inside until later, until we were out of this, finally on our home ground and safe.

We all breathed a sigh of relief when an opening, likely the last of the season, was called and Tim decided, finally, that there was no way we'd be able to fish. We'd be a blocker for our partners, the *Sea Mist* and *Rafferty*, and would run other boats away from them as they set. I'd be lowered in the rubber Zodiak to buzz around their sets, clamping buoys on the cork line. It wasn't frightening at all to be back in the fray. Just the opposite, I was exhilarated and happy to return to active life—to get out of my muddled head. To be doing anything that was not sitting around in a fog and stewing about our situation, wondering why I had been spared.

37

THE LONG VOYAGE HOME

IT WAS BOUNCY at first as the *Iliamna Bay* headed into four- or five-foot swells, but the weather wasn't particularly bad and we took our wheel watches faithfully. Conversation is always at a minimum when the motor is running, but things had fallen particularly silent. Not necessarily in a bad way. I think our spirits were buoyed by the fact that after five days—days that had dragged on as if they were years—we had finally plotted a course for home and would hopefully be there in less than a week. And sleep, when it actually came, came hard. After so many nights of deliberation, tossing and turning to questions that seemed to have no answers, it was no wonder I fell under the spell of the engine's hypnotic drone and sank into a heavy slumber. I was not only tired, but tired of thinking, and sack time seemed as good a way as any to kill the waning hours. Still, I kept thinking Tim had something to say; now with endless cruising ahead and a large stretch of time left to ponder, there seemed to be something eating at him.

We were probably well into our third day, nearly to the half-way point of our voyage—through the Aleutians and cruising along the Alaska Range—when Tim decided a break was in order.

"I need to stop," he said, "check the engine and all that, and take a walk." It was sunny as we made our way into a secluded cove and I dropped anchor. Tim was still inside when Karl, who'd been in his bunk, emerged on deck.

"What the hell are we doing?" he asked me. He was obviously annoyed. It was the first time I'd seen Karl even remotely upset.

"I don't know," I said, a little defensively. He knew it wasn't my choice. "Tim wants to take a break, check the engine," I explained. I could see his nerves were frayed, that he too was counting—as we all were—the miles, the minutes, before we made it to Homer.

Tim killed the motor. After three days of ear plugs, three days of that monotonous rumble bouncing off the inside of our skulls, the silence was deafening, soothing, and complete, and it seemed to calm Karl. It calmed us all. Soon Tim emerged on deck with a broad smile and began talking of laying over here, in this very bay. "It's good halibut fishing right over there," he said, "maybe we should try it before we head out again."

As much as he talked about beachcombing, I hadn't seen Tim head off to shore much. Even in Cook Inlet, when the boat went dry in the Paint River where it was completely safe, he'd left only briefly. But now he was anxious to head out and insisted on going alone.

He didn't return for hours, but when he did he seemed refreshed and in good spirits, announcing we had a few chores to do—some maintenance—before getting back underway. My job would be to top the hydraulic fluid off. He showed me how to access the reservoir, which was inside the cabin, and I set to removing its cover and filling it. As I returned the cover and tightened the bolts I realized the threads holding them in place were stripped and figured it was something Tim should be aware of, although he probably already was. I waited until he returned from outside, informing him of the problem more or less in passing. It couldn't be that big a deal, I thought. I assumed they'd been stripped long before, there was pressure in the system, everything worked. But I was wrong, and couldn't believe what I began to witness. His cheeks started turning crimson, the same shade as our buoys, and the veins of his neck bulged, as a sudden severe storm began rising across his entire face.

"What the hell did you do?" he screamed, the rage welling up in his eyes, enflamed and glaring at me. I'd barely heard him raise his voice in the entire time we'd been out and now he was seething, raving, pacing back and forth, fuming about the work he'd have to do, the trouble I'd caused.

"I didn't do anything," I pleaded. I could feel the fatigue, the anger, and unrest of the entire trip rising inside, building beyond my control. I immediately turned and went out on deck before I said or did something I'd be sorry for. But Tim followed me, still in a fury.

I shouted back in my own defense, "I think I'd know if I stripped them, Goddamnit."

Karl wasn't far behind and maneuvered between us, addressing Tim. "Look, he told you he didn't do it." I was thankful he was there defending me, and surprised at the edge his voice had taken. "What's the matter with you?" he continued, almost as if he were scolding Tim.

At once Tim turned and stormed back inside, leaving me standing there, stunned.

Karl immediately came over. "You know," he said, putting his arm around me, "it's just this whole thing. It's gotten to him, to all of us." I looked at him, trying to consider what he was saying. "Think about it. He almost lost his boat, he almost lost you. Any one of us could have died. What if that boom had broken when Grant was on it? He's probably just coming to terms with it." Karl was right, but at that moment all I felt was anger and betrayal. I'd grown to respect this man; what right did he have to come after me, to provoke me like that? I hadn't come to terms with anything, either. Why in the hell was he yelling at me?

I tried to steel myself before heading back inside, and when I finally did it was impossibly quiet. Tim was standing near the helm and Brad sat at the table with his nose buried in a book. When Brad looked up he nodded in what I like to think was a gesture of commiseration and solidarity, before Tim turned abruptly toward me. He still looked agitated but also a little bewildered and thankfully quite a bit calmer. "Look," he said all at once. "I'm sorry."

"I didn't strip those things," I said.

"Someone did. But that doesn't matter," he quickly added.

"It wasn't me."

"Let's just forget it," said Tim. He sounded exasperated, but paused for a moment. "God," he said then, his voice falling so that I could barely hear him as he put a hand to my shoulder, "I'm glad you're alive, that's all."

"Me too," I said, and as much as I tried to avoid it, the tears began rolling down my cheeks.

The next few days, I fell into the torpor and routine of wheel watch interspersed with looking at our plotter, at the charts, watching the distance and the clock. Many boats set their course directly for the coordinates of the Salty Dawg Saloon, a famous watering hole on the Homer spit, and the closer we came, the greater our anticipation. Whether we actually went there or not didn't matter. It was a symbol. Usually it meant the end of a successful trip. It represented freedom, a reminder of what it was like to be on land again. To be on "my time," and one's own man. Yet as we neared Homer, the slower we seemed to travel and the longer it appeared to take. What I did know was that when I reached shore there would be no turning back. This was it. I'd had my fill of boats—at least commercial ones. I was done.

Once on land I would be able to turn inward in a new way. I would find a place to debrief, find the space to figure out what was next. Or at least so I hoped. I knew that to be removed from what had occurred was the key, the only way to even begin to rise out of this stupor. I would need to examine it from afar, with a clear eye. It would take some insight, some distance, to discover what it meant and where I was going. Wherever that was, though, it would be far from the sea, and I vowed it would be someplace meaningful. I was sure of that at least.

Finally, we rounded Point Pogibshi. Soon we could spy the Homer Spit and picture its long rows of shops and the houses along the bluff outside of town. They blended into the sharp diorama of crisscrossing snow-chained mountains as the mainland streamed into view. Though it would be a couple of hours until we made port, I could feel our spirits soar. After all we'd endured, after eleven days, the anguish of waiting and the anticipation of travel, we would be there shortly; what was a couple of hours more?

I'd already told Brad I'd give him a ride north. I didn't know if he'd told Tim that he was leaving yet or not, that he was heading out of state as soon as possible and wouldn't be there for salmon season. We'd already decided which friends and what watering holes we'd visit along the way. And I'd begun thinking about what kind of retreat was in order. Maybe just a week or two at home on secure, neutral ground, with ground being the key word. It was a notion I usually reserved for the end of the season, the long rainy days at the close of fishing in Prince William Sound. That was when I'd picture myself in the most secure and comfortable place I knew, on that familiar threadbare couch in the corner of my cabin, feet propped up near the woodstove, a good book in hand and the ample luxury of time and space—plenty of space. The perfect place, really, to figure things out. I could hardly wait. That's when Tim's cell phone rang. He'd forgotten he'd even turned it on and after a month of not hearing anything even closely resembling its incongruous ring it startled us.

"Who's wife is that?" asked Karl, once he realized it was not an engine or a bilge alarm.

"Probably mine," said Tim as he began to hunt for the curious sound and scrambled to find the device.

"Hello," he shouted, juggling the phone to his ear. "What?" He appeared confused and a little annoyed, as if it were a wrong number. "Who?" It obviously wasn't his wife.

We all waited, and then he turned toward me. "It's for you," he said, holding the phone out.

"What?" I was incredulous. "Who the hell would be calling me here?"

Tim shrugged, almost in condolence as though he were thinking the same thing I was. This can't be good. *What now?* I thought. Just as we are arriving, I'm finally free and something terrible has happened. This time it might be a family member—maybe even my dad.

"Hello," I said tentatively.

"Hello," the voice on the other end came back. It wasn't a great connection, but the voice was still booming and familiar. "It's Bob."

"Bob? Bob Linville," I said, answering my own question. "What in the hell . . ."

"I need your help," he said.

"What's up?"

"I had an accident. The boat, it fell on my leg," he said. "It's broken."

"What?"

"Well, the boat's not broken, but the leg is and pretty bad. I need you to come run the *Coyote* for me."

"Oh, man," I said. "I'm not going out on any boat again, ever."

"Just call me when you get in. There's no one else."

"You don't understand," I explained. I looked at the other guys, all staring at me now, waiting for what I was going to say next. "It's been crazy out here. We had a fuckin' harrowing experience. We almost lost the boat."

He wouldn't take no for an answer. "Just call me when you get in," he insisted, "I don't know anyone else that could do it." I knew he was right—he would need to be on the boat, broken leg and all, with the way the engine and everything else was jerry-rigged—but who else could work with Bob, put up with him in such close quarters.

"There's no way," I insisted once again, but he cut me off and made me promise to call him when we reached land.

As I handed the phone back to Tim I noticed everyone still staring at me, waiting to hear what had happened. "Bob," I said, "the guy I fish with in the Sound. He broke his leg, wants me to come run his boat out there."

"What did you tell him?" asked Karl.

"You heard me," I said emphatically. "Fishing opens Tuesday, four days from now. No way. I'm not going out there. I'm not going anywhere on a boat again, ever." I paused for a second or two to reflect on this, on my friend's dilemma, and then added regretfully, "I really don't know what he's going to do."

38

NEW BEGINNINGS

ONCE TIM DISMISSED us, that's when I first began to experience it. I always feel relief after a trip, a slow return to normalcy, back to real life—whatever that is. But this was completely different. It was immediate and building with each step up the dock and onto dry land, as if I were blithely floating above it all. It was a buoyancy, a vitality I'd never experienced or imagined possible. As I passed strangers, tourists, other fishermen, I felt like telling each of them my story, hugging them, shouting out as I swung them around in gratitude. A new lease on life, they call it. I'd heard the expression carelessly bandied around before, but now I knew exactly what it meant. I had one. I could do anything, go anywhere, and I would.

Brad was as giddy as I was and as promised I gave him a ride north. Making various stops along the way, neither of us wanted to rehash what had happened, just sharing enough, so that friends knew what we were telling them was important, that it had changed our lives, even though we didn't know exactly how yet. I also called Bob and told him the same thing, enough that he'd give me a few days at least before we would talk again.

While I was gone winter had definitely passed; the aroma of budding alder and wildflowers seemed to permeate the air, replacing the cold emptiness of the bygone season with life and vitality. Whether in town or along the trail behind my cabin, the signs of the new season, of rejuvenation and rebirth, were all around me, and with them all the locals—my neighbors and friends—had come out from their lairs, busy with chores of all kinds: hauling out the old, clearing winter's refuse, and planning anew. Wherever I went, though, I felt a step behind, in no hurry. While everyone else was emerging, I was longing to den up—if just for a short while. I would manage it, to create that distance, if only for a few days. I'd at least attempt to shore myself up, gather my aimless mish-mash of thoughts, though I'd hardly had enough time to even begin sorting them out.

Through the haze, however, an inkling of something important had surfaced. In my mind I kept going back to people I'd met, older people, who had told me again and again how time had accelerated as they aged. And how the realization of how short life was, how little time they had left, became more acute. It was a notion easily dismissed by a young man, but one that suddenly and startlingly had come into view. Despite my lack of years I'd reached a threshold, or been pushed toward one, bluntly crashing into the realization that time was no longer in excess. Oh, I still saw the importance of making time for reflection, as I had at Exit Glacier—as I was doing at that very moment—but I was well aware that I'd also been granted a not-so-subtle reminder of how life was finite, and that I must do something with it and make the most of it. Part of that, at least in the short-term, was helping a friend in need.

I'd have to get ready quickly, do a few chores myself. I would even stumble upon a member of the *Sea Mist* crew while having my tires changed. It was Greg, and I didn't even recognize him. We'd been through hell, working together for twelve hours, stood next to each other in the skiff, in terror, thinking the *Iliamna Bay* was going down, and I nearly passed him by.

Unfortunately, I was never able to meet up with Brad again. I regretted leaving him that first evening on shore, after dropping him off with just a brief goodbye, our plans to go trout fishing and camping now unexpectedly scuttled. Though it seemed inadequate,

I called him and explained that it was one of those unavoidable detours, and that it had simply gotten in the way. Wow, he said, he couldn't believe it, his shock, his utter disbelief, quite apparent when I explained to him that I'd be helping Bob launch the *Coyote* and then heading to Cordova within the next few days.

We missed the first opening, but by the second—only a handful of days after arriving home from Bristol Bay—I would find myself cloistered with Bob on the *Coyote*, where I'd finally recount the whole story for him. I also kept telling myself, through that strange sense of euphoria, that it was good to be getting back out there, back on the horse and all that. Someone told me that this lingering contentment where nothing seemed to bother me was a form of Post-Traumatic Stress Disorder. If so, I said, let me have it. But inside I immediately reconsidered my statement. *At what price?* I thought.

Whatever it was, however, it had found me. This unfamiliar yet welcome feeling of calm transcendence would continue to hover in varying degrees over the next six to eight months. It would follow me setnetting later in the summer, where there was ample time to reflect between openings—even during openings—through the long hours of picking fish and afterwards, through the mundane and meditative act of hanging nets. I had even begun to make some decisions. I didn't know what the future held, whether I'd fish next year or not. I'd finish the season though. Somehow I had also managed to bankroll nearly forty thousand dollars, a fortune for someone like me. But money had never really meant that much and now it meant even less. More important—much more important—was health, in a holistic sense, and the spiritual and mental wellbeing that accompanies it, as well as the ability to somehow share it. Suddenly, if I couldn't do something to effect change, to make a difference, even in passing, what was the point? But who knew where to begin. There were so many without a voice, the downtrodden of the Earth—perhaps the Earth itself, even the fish I was catching.

Even here in Alaska, many of them were in trouble. But perhaps I would start with something less drastic, something just as important but within reach—working with kids maybe, or even helping a neighbor. I didn't know what it was or where but I'd find it. I'd do something with the time I had left. I would do my best to not squander the gift of a second chance.

EPILOGUE

MY DRIVE BEGAN on one of those rare, absolutely gorgeous days of early winter. Windless and unseasonably warm. Difficult to believe that it was approaching 2013—nearly sixteen years since the incident on the *Iliamna Bay* and almost twice that since I'd first arrived in Seward and set sail on the *Lancer*. Living little more than an hour's drive from Seward I'd spent a lot of time there over the years, usually traveling there for fun—to go sport fishing or to visit the Linvilles. But now, nearly three decades later, I was heading to Seward for an entirely different reason. This time I was trying to track down Mark.

As I drove through the mountain pass from my home in Sterling, from the cabin I still lived in and had spent the years fixing up, I tried not to be nervous or plan too much. I'd figure out what to say, what to ask; I'd just let it come.

When I began looking for him I started with databases and court records, but hadn't gotten anywhere. I only knew that he might have been in Michigan. When a friend, a private investigator, heard I was going to spend thirty dollars on one of those internet searches, he immediately told me to hang on, to save my money and let him try. He'd find Mark. It was his business after all.

I was surprised when only a day or two later he called and in typical *CSI* fashion, told me, "I found your man."

"Already?" I asked. I was shocked. How could that be?

When he told me Mark was in Seward my shock immediately fell into disbelief.

"Impossible," I protested. "After thirty years? If he'd been there all this time I would have known."

"People return to places that are familiar," he said, "even after thirty years."

"You're positive?" I asked again.

"Finding people is what I do," he assured me. "At least that's where he was a couple months ago, I guarantee it."

"And murder . . .?" I finally asked.

"Nope, at least never convicted. That doesn't mean he wasn't questioned. He's had a lot of run-ins, mostly minor stuff. Nothing like murder. But you might want to be careful," he added, leaving it at that and turning over an address.

So here I was, the tourists long gone, with the road to myself and in no hurry. But who was I kidding? I was purposely taking my time, especially as I reached the outskirts of Seward and slowly began following a series of gravel roads to the address. When I arrived I found a pair of long buildings that inside reminded me of construction trailers—the type that temporarily house workers on a remote site. The buildings had been more or less permanently planted and haphazardly covered in rough-cut wood siding. There were a few houses on the outskirts, but there seemed to be no one around. The place was completely devoid of people—only a lonely dog's moaning carried over the valley on a slight breeze. There was definitely a weird, end-of-the-world vibe hanging in the air as I stepped out of my truck and surveyed the situation. Maybe this was what I had expected, but not what I had hoped to find. I'd hoped he'd have settled into a homey apartment with a nice woman. But as I entered the first structure and followed the paint-chipped walls I knew that wasn't likely to be the case. My shoes tapped a hollow echo that only added to the suspense as I approached an apartment at the end of the hall, its door ajar, lights on and radio blaring. I felt like a gumshoe in a cheap detective movie, calling out a cavernous hello—a scene replayed a million times where the detective meets his untimely demise at the hands of any variety of felon or fanatic. When no one called back I continued my search. I entered the next building and stopped at the sound of a television from apartment number four, the one where Mark supposedly lived. I paused before the door. I felt like just turning around and hightailing it out of there, but I forced a tentative knock. "Just a minute," a voice called. It was a man's voice, somewhat annoyed, and as I heard footsteps approaching the door my heart began to palpitate wildly. The door swung open, first a crack and then suddenly wide.

I was immediately relieved and disappointed. Though about the right age, this was not the man I had known. Right off I asked if he had heard of or knew Mark. The man, slightly balding, wearing a robe and colorful socks, initially seemed overly suspicious. "What do you want him for?" He was defensive. Maybe he thought I really was a cop. But as I began to explain the situation, that it had been thirty years since I'd seen Mark and that we'd worked together "back in the day," he began to loosen up. He told me that Mark had indeed lived there, in that very room, "a stray," much like himself, taken in by the owner of the place. I eventually told him I was writing about those times and he explained that he too was a writer, but more of an investigative journalist. I initially didn't detect anything amiss about him or his story, other than his being a stray. But there are a lot of us out there. Maybe he'd made a choice to be one. After all, it wasn't that uncommon in Alaska. He seemed like a nice enough guy, a little quirky, eccentric, that's it. I'd worked with a lot of these types over the years. But as he relaxed and loosened up, and as I began to take a closer look around his room, with its faux wood paneling and stacks of books, I began to wonder. Along with an old manual typewriter stationed on a desk in the corner, there were large tomes, most of which, as far as I could make out, were about the CIA and the government. Finally he even confided in me that until about six months ago he'd been hearing voices. That's right, voices, out of the blue, and now that he wasn't hearing them any longer, he said, it was as if emerging from a dark bar into the lightness of day.

That's when I knew it was time to make my getaway. But I still needed to find out what he knew about Mark.

"You don't look like someone that might be hunting for him," he said at one point. "I don't know what he means to you, so don't want to say anything bad about him." Again, I explained that it had been thirty years, that I'd been young, and that I didn't necessarily expect much. That's when he told me Mark had been hired as the handyman, but had been run off a few months before. He suggested, much like my friend the investigator, that maybe I didn't really want to find him. "To tell you the truth," he eventually confided in me, "he's no good." And this was coming from a guy who, though it was no fault of his own, heard voices.

I breathed a heavy sigh of relief when I finally made my exit. But before I left my new friend had given me a few leads, including the number of the woman who owned the place—the one who took in all the strays. She explained to me that like a lot of people, Mark probably just had his demons. And while she may have had to ask him to leave they were still in touch and though they hadn't talked in a month or so, she gave me his cell number. She believed he'd decided to head back to Michigan, but wasn't sure if it was for good or just for the holidays. I wondered how a guy who had been kicked out of a place like this had even found the money to travel, and I was surprised for some reason that he even had a cell phone.

Each time I called, however, I had to admit to feeling a bit of relief, listening to the message that this user was out of range, and then later that the phone was no longer in service. Maybe his whereabouts and fate were better left alone. At least that's what everyone kept telling me.

I'd never head to Seward without at least dropping in on the Linvilles. After hearing my story, Bob agreed with everyone else that finding Mark was perhaps not the best idea. The large place Bob and Patty had built seemed a bit empty, the kids being grown and out of the house. The two boys, in their mid-twenties, had each started fishing; before they were even out of high school, they were the owners of their own drift boats and were permit holders. Today, the oldest, Gus, skippers a seiner and his sister Annie occasionally crews for him. His younger brother Bobby fishes the Copper River flats out of Cordova in his drift boat.

Bob had had some difficult years, but I was happy to see him doing well. He had taken ill in the early 1990s, not long after I had started working for the family, with a slight weakness and inflammation that doctors could not initially pinpoint. It hadn't appeared so bad then, but as it grew progressively worse it was difficult for me to see someone so full of vigor and determination slowly losing his strength and struck down by some mysterious illness. If it could happen to him it could happen to anyone.

Through the rest of the decade he tried a multitude of alternative therapies, which would stabilize his condition for varying periods. They finally diagnosed it as something called Aplastic Anemia. It's a condition where the stem cells that reside in the bone marrow are damaged, and as a last resort a bone marrow transplant is attempted. Unfortunately, on top of everything else, when they were suffering the worst of this disease, Bob and Patty were forced to sue their insurance company. "If they think you are going to die," Bob said at one point, "they'll deny it until you're gone."

Fortunately, the family prevailed, forcing the company to pay for the procedure before it was too late. "That was the worst time," said Bob, referring to 2005, when he finally received the transplant and had to undergo chemotherapy and endure the side effects of both that and the transplant. Yet in all that time, though he had lost a substantial amount of weight, zapped of his strength, his energy depleted, I never once saw him lose his spirit. "It was the family that mainly kept me going," he says today, "the kids were in school and involved in those activities and in fishing, and I wanted to be there for them."

With the boys more interested in owning their own boats, the Linvilles figured it best to sell the setnet operation, which they did in 2006. It was still a money maker—still is—but without the family, it wasn't the same. "Of course, it was never really about the money," said Bob, "it was all about the family, the lifestyle, and living out there."

By 2007, seventeen years after he had taken ill, Bob finally began to feel better. Today he is completely recovered. He even returned to fish a couple of summers, confiding in me that the first time he retrieved the net on his drift boat it was full of fish, and that after spending seven hours picking it, he decided he would not lay it out again. *The gentleman fisherman*. We both had a good laugh over that, such an un-Bob-like thing to do or be.

It is rare when we get together that we don't share a good laugh or reminisce at least a little about our time spent in Main Bay—agreeing it was some of the best years of our lives. While he is done with the day-to-day ritual of fishing, Bob does still work with the kids in an advisory role, partnering with Gus in the design of a new seiner that is being built in Homer and should be on the water by 2015.

When I'm in Seward I can't help picturing those first days, when I arrived so raw and untested, reminiscing about how things used to be, and counting all the ways the place has changed. The waterfront has been built up, the tourist trade is booming, and there seems to be fewer old-time fishermen around—those guys that cut such imposing figures in my youth. Woody, unfortunately, passed away in 2010. I often wished I had gone to see him as an adult, approached him on some sort of equal footing. I was sure there was more to him than I'd seen on the *Lancer*. Not just the screamer, but the man I occasionally caught a glimpse of, the one who unexpectedly gave me the treatise on "Tortilla Flat," for example, or who a dozen years later composed an ode to his true friend and partner Mr. Sanchez—paying homage to his life and commemorating his death in an obituary-style article he placed in the local paper.

I did, however, have the opportunity to discuss his later days with his onetime friend, Jim Pruitt, a longtime fixture in Seward. He described his first meeting with Woody in the 1970s. It was as crazy a meeting as one would expect from those rough and tumble times, and from someone like Darwin Wood.

Jim found Woody—apparently always quite the drinker—nearly passed out at a local watering hole. He and another fellow decided to be good Samaritans and volunteered to see that Woody made it home. The woman he was living with apparently was not very happy to see his condition and as she began to rant about it, Woody emerged from the bedroom where he'd been placed, still quite drunk and with a pistol in hand. He began firing, shooting errantly, mostly into a nearby sofa. Jim, having counted five shots, cajoled Woody into firing once more before wrestling the gun free, only to discover that instead of a six-shooter it was a nine-shooter. Despite the gunplay, the two emerged as close friends. They'd even traveled to Belize together, and Woody was often invited to Jim's home to share holidays with his family.

But as he'd gotten older, Woody had apparently grown extremely bitter. The consensus among the old timers I talked to seemed to be that he had a falling out with just about everyone—even those who at one time had cared about him. He was his own worst enemy, I was told, always believing there was some big conspiracy, someone out to get him. It was something I saw as I began to look back at the letters to the editor he wrote on what Jim referred to as his old Royal Unabomber typewriter. They seemed to start out almost farcical, eruditely poking fun at the city council and local government, but over the years they grew extremely vehement and pointed. In the end he'd ostracized all his old friends, including his only brother, who, Jim said, thought the world of him.

Early on, though, Woody had been well liked, and everyone agrees he loved kids—something I initially found difficult to believe, but which after reconsidering, I could see. He liked the innocent, or those he perceived as innocent—the dogs and the kids of the world. And when the neighborhood children would stop by and comment on how sick he looked he would tell them he was seasick, which usually meant a hangover.

Unfortunately by the end, many of his personal relationships had deteriorated so much that no one stepped forward to claim his body. Jim, who'd had a falling out with him long before, says that because he was out of the country he didn't find out until a few years later; otherwise, despite their differences, he certainly would have seen to it that Woody had a proper burial. He was a good guy, a good friend at one time, and certainly quite a character.

My next opportunity to find Mark came purely by chance. Rarely do I even glance at the police beat in the local paper, but a few months after that first trip to Seward in search of Mark, I was scrolling through the section and the news just popped out at me. He'd been picked up on an outstanding warrant along the Seward Highway. It was March and despite the still frosty temperatures he had been sleeping under a tarp near Anchorage and had apparently been remanded to the Anchorage jail. Unfortunately the paper was a few days old, and when I contacted the jail I found that he'd been released on "unsupervised probation." This time my friend the investigator had nothing. If someone doesn't have a phone or address and their probation is unsupervised, they could be anywhere, he informed me. Once again he suggested I drop my search. "No good can come of this," he warned. At this point I figured he was right. If we were meant to meet we would. Besides, I'd been young and impressionable when we'd taken to the sea for our adventure aboard the *Lancer*. I'd looked up to him then as we walked the streets together, tough and impervious; maybe, rather than being let down, it was better to keep it that way, knowing him as I still did now, fondly and in memory.

Brad Doran, my crewmate on the *Iliamna Bay* was not nearly so difficult to find. I called him out of the blue not long ago. After leaving Alaska he had almost immediately found a job in audio engineering, which he'd trained for in college, and for eight or nine years he'd worked in the field, even building software used by the recording industry. Later on, having come from what he called a construction family, he began his own construction business; that was about the time he was beginning his own family too. He now lives with his wife and kids in the San Francisco Bay Area, and he says he often thinks about Alaska, his time fishing, and that transformative night that he too maintains has made him all the more appreciative of what he has. He also said he plans on getting back to Alaska some day. Who knows, we may even make that trout fishing trip yet.

My other deck mate, Karl Kircher, still lives with his family in the area and I run into him quite often. Not long after our voyage together, he returned to school. He received his teaching credentials and after several years in the classroom as a respected educator is now the principal of a local school. He still has his fishing sites and spends the summer setnetting with his family in Cook Inlet.

Greg Gabriel, deckhand on the *Sea Mist* and last off the *Iliamna Bay* that night, also still lives in the area. He's now a lawyer, specializing in—what else?—fishery issues, and he still finds the time to spend his summers seining for salmon in Prince William Sound.

Butch Schollenberg still owns the *Sea Mist* while very successfully continuing to fish the Sound. He also remains a part of Tim's radio group, sharing information and often traveling together to various openings.

Not long after that night Grant Henderson, skipper of the *Rafferty*, sold his boat. He says it had nothing to do with what happened, that it was more the financial uncertainty of fishing that led to his decision. "It was just so up and down, it was hard to know how I was going to provide for my family." He worked with computers for a couple of companies before returning to school and becoming an operator in the oil fields on Alaska's North Slope. But after a life of fishing, it's in his blood and he found it hard to say no when a friend proposed he fish his vessel in the summer of 2010. The friend wanted Grant to take his teenage son along and show him the ropes. Grant brought his own son as well, and that was it. The next year he took the summer off from his oil field job and was once again fishing his own boat.

Tim Moore, to this day the consummate fisherman, sold the *Iliamna Bay* in 2003, replacing it with the *Marandah*—a much larger, state-of-the-art vessel. The name *Marandah* is what Tim calls a "customized mixture" of his kids' initials. He has a son and three daughters, some of whom still occasionally crew on their namesake vessel. There is not an instance when Tim and I meet up that we don't discuss, at least a little bit, that fateful night. And each time he seems to invariably bring up that afternoon on our return voyage and those stripped fittings, always profusely apologizing for getting so angry over it. "I know it wasn't you, I remember now the guy that did it. It must have just been the pressure, it built up and finally got to me." Of course, I have never held Tim in anything but the highest regard and greatest respect. He is the fisherman's fisherman, and one of the safest and best captains I ever worked for. And I always assure him it's water long under the bridge.

As for me, change never did come in one fell swoop as it seemed it would on the dock that afternoon as I left the *Iliamna Bay*. It did eventually arrive, but as the euphoria—the PTSD if that's what it was—wore off, it manifested itself more slowly. Change came in small doses. I knew an evolution of sorts had begun taking place; I just wasn't sure where it was leading me. I fished another season with the Linvilles and continued to work outdoors seasonally for the Alaska Department of Fish and Game and as a freelance writer, working mostly on sport fishing and hunting articles.

The idea of volunteerism, of giving back in some way, had been instilled in me early. The ideal of pursuing at least a somewhat contemplative life was important too. Yet there had always been an inherent conflict, where society's deeply ingrained notions of success and status had come up hard against those more spiritual notions of humility. Even the virtue found in attempting to help others, or in the case of the earth, helping everyone, often comes under suspicion— because whether grand or simple, these are acts that most likely will never prove profitable. They can even sometimes be viewed, as trifling, especially in the case of contemplation. And if we are talking about action, such as environmental action—which should be undertaken by every fisher, commercial or sport, each and every hunter, and all lovers of the great outdoors—it can even be met with contempt by a large number of our fellow citizens. But I have no doubt that it was the events that night on the *Iliamna Bay,* and perhaps seeing Bob struck down and later rebound from illness, that reminded me of what was important. They pushed me in a certain direction and went a long way in allowing me to overcome any feelings of reproach I may have experienced in pursuing a different path. I considered myself lucky, though it hardly seemed so at the time, to have received a reminder of how tenuous life is, and when I was still so young.

Initially, it was difficult to find that place where I might make a difference. I volunteered during the off season on various projects, including helping to construct a building that would house the local food bank, which was run for several years by Peggy Moore, Tim's wife. But ultimately it was nature—my church and the place I found true refuge—that called.

As life would have it, this was about the same time I stumbled upon this quote by Wendell Berry:

". . . the care of the earth is our most ancient and most worthy and, after all, our most pleasing responsibility. To cherish what remains of it, and to foster its renewal, is our only legitimate hope."

This was also about the time I began hearing about a project that was being proposed for Western Alaska. It was said that this proposed endeavor might become the largest open-pit mine in North America or maybe even the world, and it was being planned right here in Bristol Bay—so near to my home, and at the head-waters of the greatest wild salmon fishery left on the planet. We'd long ago screwed up the salmon fisheries in Europe, and later the East Coast of the United States, before significantly depleting them along the Pacific Northwest. I was astounded to learn that 350 runs of wild salmon had gone extinct in the Pacific Northwest, and many of those within my lifetime. What was left? My beloved Alaska, of course. I'd seen what had happened to Prince William Sound after the *Exxon Valdez* oil spill: the herring have never recovered. And as I learned more about this project, called the Pebble Mine, the worse it sounded. Jobs for twenty, maybe thirty years in exchange for the last runs of wild sockeyes, and a pit of toxic waste left for future generations to tend in perpetuity. It seemed like a bum deal all the way around and I vowed to dedicate a year of my life, my full attention and effort, to fighting it. I volunteered and later worked for several of the groups attempting to protect this amazing fishery and the land I loved. I stuck with it for nearly three years, before finally having to take a step back—battle-scarred and weary.

It was an interesting time as well as an often maddening one. I found that the captains of industry and their minions—many of whom they've placed into key positions in government—have the advantage of unlimited resources. They have the capacity to hire an army that advances one after the other. These people, however, don't take the fight home with them. They don't wake up in the middle of the night worrying about it, wondering what they might do to affect its outcome—because for them it's not really a full-time fight, and that's their advantage. For them it's just a job, and there's always someone to take their place. An onslaught in opposition to the impassioned few.

As in the past, I learned from experience. Like fishing, I found that it takes a lot of nerve, to stand up for what you believe in, but it's a different kind of nerve. It takes courage to be heard, to get in front of an audience or to a greater degree be embroiled in a public discourse and actual debate. And in that debate I discovered in many instances that genuine passion and sincerity, focused in the right way, will often trump slick, professional polish and even money.

But as so often happens when one is engrossed in a battle, I had forgotten something vital. It is advice that can be heard in the words of activist and writer Edward Abbey, who said that while it is important to be an enthusiast and a crusader, that it's also important to save the other half of yourself for pleasure and adventure. "It is not enough to fight for the land; it is even more important to enjoy it. While you can. While it is still here."

I have heeded his advice, and no matter how difficult, know that we must occasionally step back. I still work to protect both the land and the water, with groups like Trout Unlimited, and write about conservation issues whenever I can, but I also remember to reserve some of my most precious time for the all-important and revitalizing act of contemplation. For if we are truly to be a product of our experiences, we must take the time to heed their message. It is because of my experiences that I am a bit more grateful than I once was for everyday pleasures; I can appreciate moments of introspection even more, and most importantly I am reminded that no day is guaranteed. As nerve has taken its logical, timely course, and that turbulent petulant nerve of youth has been replaced by confidence and hopefully at least a small modicum of wisdom, I now no longer must prove myself in the wild, but instead must do what I can, even in the smallest way, to preserve it.

It is a difficult balance, to find the strength to fight but also to appreciate the wonder of this land, held in its towering mountains and pristine streams, its sheer beauty and its great spirit, before which I often find myself rendered expressionless. Alaska may have at times kicked my ass, but in the process it has taught me a great deal. And as I look back, from this vantage point I know Karl was right that night on the deck as we surveyed our damaged boat: what doesn't kill you, if you let it, may just make you stronger.

ACKNOWLEDGMENTS

I WOULD FIRST LIKE to thank the crew of the *Iliamna Bay,* Tim Moore, Karl Kircher, and Brad Doran, as well as Greg Gabriel, Grant Henderson and Butch Schollenberg, for their time and their willingness to be interviewed. Also a big thank you to the Linvilles, Bob and Patty, for allowing me to share their, and our, story. I would also like to thank the editors at Skyhorse, Jay Cassell and especially Constance Renfrow for all their hard work. Also a great deal of appreciation goes to those friends and colleagues who took the time to read and comment on early versions of the book: Jeanette Pedginski, Cindy Detrow, Robb Justice, Kristin DeSmith, and especially Susan Nabholz.